The Rhine River Cruise

Eight Days of Passion and Adventure

Ruben Reyes

Table of Contents

Introduction

"The air grows cool and dark; the Rhine flows calmly on; the mountain summit sparkles in the light of the setting sun" (Dana, 1869, p. 553). These words, written by the 19th-century German poet Heinrich Heine, show the reverence those in Europe have afforded the Rhine River for centuries. The river has been a quintessential part of not only German but European history. It has proved itself the one constant in the region, having never been destroyed by wars and other calamities that befell the nations surrounding it. Although history has run its course on the banks of the Rhine, the waters have continued to flow to say, "Do not fear." It has been the birthplace of many myths and stories concocted by its surrounding citizens. One German legend claims that hundreds of years ago, a beautiful woman threw herself into the Rhine after discovering the unfaithfulness of her partner. Today, she is said to have transformed into a siren behind a rock—known as *Lorelei*—that calls fishermen to destruction. Although no evidence has ever been found concerning the validity of this story, it portrays the deep roots the Rhine has in European culture and folklore. The Rhine River begins high in the Alps of Switzerland and flows an estimated 820 miles through various countries until it reaches the

Netherlands and drains in the area. Today, the Rhine is still a mode of transport that is utilized by various industries. Additionally, it is the home of many tourists who cruise through the region. The fleet that travels on the Rhine accounts for no less than 6,900 vessels (Mavrokefalidis, 2022)!

Many vessels that constitute this enormous fleet are classified as river cruise boats. River cruises have become a pastime for many tourists who want to travel Europe in luxury. Most of these vessels are hotels on the water, with spacious staterooms, grand dining rooms, and onboard activities. They are especially prevalent on the Rhine due to the abundance of castles and other historical structures along its banks. These cruises can last from a couple of days to weeks, depending on what the visitor wants to experience. A specific vessel that offers a great experience is the Viking Tialfi. The layout of this vessel is spacious and allows for phenomenal views of the area as it glides majestically through the water. It was this boat that housed Ruben and Adora—together with Pol and Ruby—on their trip. Given that Ruben is in the United States Navy, he thought he knew all there is to know concerning water travel. However, his cruise on the Rhine opened his eyes to the splendor of Europe from the windows of a luxury vessel. Furthermore, it was the perfect opportunity for Ruben to pursue his relationship with Adora. Their eight-day cruise, and various stops along the way, strengthened their relationship and opened Adora's eyes to Ruben's absolute affection and love for her. Their eight days of passion and adventure were to be remembered for years to come. Join Ruben, Adora, Pol, and Ruby on their trip on the Rhine. It was surely unforgettable.

Chapter 1:

Let's Go on a Cruise

On a cold Sunday morning, Ruben sat in church. The day had started like any other. He went to the mess hall for breakfast, took a shower, and thought of what to wear. He decided upon a blue dress shirt and black slacks. As he drove to church, he had no idea that the day would prove to be like no other. When he walked in, he found that his usual spot had been taken, and he opted to sit in a pew located at the back of the church. An elderly lady was seated next to him. He had seen her before but never engaged in a conversation. "Thank you for your service," she said. How did she know that he was in the Navy? Perhaps another member of the congregation told her about his profession. Ruben replied with a reserved, "Thank you for your support." The pastor made his way to the pulpit and began the service. The topic was the Book of James, and the congregation grabbed their Bibles, frantically paging to locate the verse under discussion. Ruben forgot his bible at the barracks and looked at the congregation, trying to notice anyone who looked familiar. His eyes befell on a young woman who he had never seen before. He was instantly mesmerized. She wore a long floral dress and seemed to flick her black hair bashfully every time the pastor said "Amen." Ruben considered asking his elderly neighbor what her name was but chose to ask the attention-grabbing young lady after the service. He wondered what she'd think when a strange man approaches her. Yet, he swallowed his pride and convinced himself that it was worth it.

When the service ended, Ruben remained in his pew and planned how he'll strike up a conversation without seeming awkward. He knew he didn't want to seem shy or scare her off. As she walked down the aisle towards the majestic oak doors, he stood up and followed her outside. She was with a young man and woman but seemed the odd one out, standing a distance from her two friends who shared a laugh. He made eye contact. When she looked at him, his heart was beating, accompanied by a flush of heat through his entire body. His cheeks felt warm, but her coy smile intrigued him and led his steps toward her. He heard himself say "Hi," and she responded in kind. Her voice was soothing and put him at peace. "I've never seen you here before, are you a new member?" he asked in a soft tone. "Yes," she answered, "my friends have been going to this church for the past year and invited me to come with them today." Her companions seemed uninterested in this strange man talking to their friend. Ruben did not care. They spoke for 10 minutes. With every passing moment, he could feel himself falling for her. Her invested input in the conversation was a sign that his efforts were successful. Her name was Adora. Her two friends beckoned her to end the interaction and go for waffles. She introduced them as Pol and Ruby. They seemed nice but Ruben's focus was solely on the enchanting Adora.

As her Pol attempted to pull her away, Ruben was urged to ask for her number. He was nervous that this was a step too far but asked anyway. To his amazement, Adora retrieved a pen and paper from her purse and jotted down her number. Ruben couldn't believe his luck and promised to text her as soon as he got home. She gave him a hug and walked away with her friends. Her floral dress was blowing in the wind, and Ruben was convinced that he had found the woman he wanted to spend the rest of his life with.

Back in the barracks in Jacksonville, he made haste to text Adora. He pondered about what to say and decided on a clear message that showed his keen interest and opened the door for further encounters. "It was nice meeting you; would you like to meet for a coffee next week?" Although Ruben knew she seemed friendly, he was still the picture of anxiety as he waited for her response. A few minutes later, his phone lit up, and he closed one eye as if he was scared to face her reply. He need not have worried. "It was nice meeting you too, I would definitely want to see you again!" Ruben could not bury his excitement and did a small dance as his fellow serviceman, Mark, looked on in confusion. Three days later, Ruben and Adora met up at a local coffee shop. She was even more beautiful than he remembered. As she spoke, he looked at her with admiration. Adora talked about her job as a nurse and informed him that she lived with her aunt, Tess. Tess has always played a big role in her life, and she would not consider any big decision without counseling her aunt first. Ruben talked to her about his experiences in the Navy. He told her a few funny stories of his journeys, and she said she'd always wanted to go on a cruise. They bonded over similar interests in cruising and healthcare. The conversation soon shifted to the majesty of the ocean and water travel. Adora mentioned the quote by Brooks Atkinson, "Land was created for boats to visit" (Perry, 2013, p. 24). He asked her whether she would ever like to go on a cruise, and she responded with a resounding "Yes!" Ruben almost asked her to join him on a cruise but concluded that it might seem forward and obnoxious on a first date. As soon as the date started, it ended. Unbeknownst to her, Ruben was actively thinking about a cruise to pursue the relationship. With a long hug and a kiss on the cheek, they parted ways. Both knew that this was only their first adventure.

In time, they texted endlessly and made sure to call each other every evening. With every phone call, they seemed to get closer, and love ensued. Ruben was, however, called on a deployment to the North Sea that would last six months. Adora was saddened by this news but appreciated the service he gave to their country. He promised her that he'll try and call her every day while overseas. He did just that. He could not get Adora out of his mind and looked across the ocean, waiting to be reunited with her in a few months. Similarly, Adora missed him terribly and hoped that he would come back as he had been before. The six-month deployment felt like a year. Nevertheless, Ruben pondered their conversation regarding cruises and used their time apart to think about ways to bring her dream of a cruise to fruition. He spent many evenings doing research on cruises around the world. For a time, he wondered whether they should go on a glacier cruise or perhaps a Panama Canal cruise close to home. Because they both lived in Florida, he was drawn toward the possibility of a European cruise. That way, they'll be on the water, and he will give her the opportunity to see a new continent. Europe is often described as the continent where love is cultivated and strengthened. The perfect location for him to meet his objectives with Adora. While scrolling online, Ruben came across an article about the Rhine River. The article showed a wide array of photos of the Rhine and gave some history of the countries on which the Rhine rests its banks. He was convinced that a Rhine cruise was the way to go. He decided that he would ask her to join him once back in Florida, whereafter he could start organizing the trip.

On the day he got back to Florida, Adora was waiting for him at the port. Even before disembarking, he saw her standing on the harbor. She seemed fascinated by the ship and investigated each porthole and feature of the gigantic ship. This further ingratiated the idea that she would love a cruise on the Rhine. She met him with open arms, and they shared a kiss while Ruben held his heavy luggage in both hands. She chose to join him in a hotel three miles from the harbor, and they spent the evening drinking champagne and indulging in the many stories of Ruben's foreign adventures. The next morning, he asked her whether she would go with him on a summer cruise in Europe. For a moment she hesitated. "We're going to have to ask Tess." Ruben expected this response and was ready to ask her aunt for permission. "Maybe we could invite Pol and Ruby?" followed. This surprised Ruben, but he understood that she needed some companions to join them in a faraway land. When Ruben took Adora home later that day, he asked Tess for permission to take her beloved Adora away for a while. Tess seemed a tad uncomfortable with the proposition but assured him she'd think it over and let him know. Ruben was saddened but hopeful. He thought that Tess would realize the opportunity for Adora to break free from Florida and tour the world. Fortunately, his hopes were realized that evening. Adora texted him and said Tess agreed to let her go. Pol and Ruby also agreed to go and were just as animated as she was to embark on a European journey.

As soon as their attendance was confirmed, Ruben set to work planning the vacation. There were so many websites that offered Rhine cruises that he was at first confused as to which cruise the group would go on. He questioned whether he would plan the vacation separately, meaning purchasing airline tickets on his own and organizing travel once they arrived. Or whether he would look for an opportunity that was all-inclusive. While browsing, he saw an advertisement for a 21-day cruise on the Rhine. This piqued his interest, but he was quick to decline the offer once he saw how much it cost. Rhine cruises fluctuate in price depending on the type of ticket one takes and where the cabin is situated on the vessel. The average cost one could expect to pay is $2000 to $8000 per person (Viking River Cruises, n.d.). A certain travel website stood out to him: Viking. Their deals seemed the best, and they included airfare, together with complimentary meals and free guided tours. He was convinced that this travel agency was the way to go. He read up on the different cabin options and the routes each river cruise took. The cruise, named Rhine Getaway, was perfect. It lasted for eight days, included four countries, and had six guided tours at various stops. Ruben wondered when the best time to go would be. Did the group want to see snow? Or would they enjoy a warm, summer excursion more? As he clicked around, looking at their wide array of offers, summer was the obvious answer. He thought about holding Adora on the deck, drinking champagne, and admiring the breathtaking sunsets.

After a call with Adora, he made haste to book the tickets. The couple opted for a veranda cabin. This included a room with a double bed, a private bathroom, and a balcony where they could sit and enjoy the views. The cost for Ruben and Adora was $3,399 per person for the room, including the complimentary add-ons the trip offers. Those who book with Viking have special offers with regards to airfare, and the couple were to pay

$599 each for their plane tickets. Ruben wondered whether this was a hefty price. But seeing that accommodation, food, tours, and a range of other amenities were paid for, it seemed like a bargain. He texted Pol to tell him that he booked the tickets and let him know how the process works. Ruben was willing to pay for him and Adora, but Pol and Ruby had to pay their own way if they wanted to join. Pol went online and chose the standard stateroom with a price tag of $2,299 for him and Ruby selectively. Although the room was not as luxurious as that of Ruben and Adora, he figured that they would not spend as much time in their cabin in any case. He read that the vessel had many open areas on deck and thought the cabin was merely an area for them to lay their heads at night. They would also be required to pay $599 for their airfare. After their tickets were booked, they could not wait. In a month's time, they would be sipping cocktails overlooking the banks of the Rhine.

Nevertheless, some admin had to be sorted out. Luckily for the group, United States citizens do not need a visa to enter the European Union; that is, if they spend less than 30 days in the region. They all had passports, so the process was easy. All they had to do was collect their tickets and pack for the cruise. The cruise was to take place on June 26th and end on July 3rd. "The weather is going to be perfect," Adora told Ruben. Ruben did all the research he could on the various stops and the vessel they would be taking. The Viking Tialfi was to be their home at the end of June. He couldn't help but look at images of the vessel whenever he had the chance. Ruben had seen many ships in his lifetime, but the structure of the Tialfi was intriguing. The entire half of the ship, it looked like, was entirely out of glass. The elongated formation was like a hotel on water and his excitement couldn't be dampened when he read that they would be offered entertainment on board. He knew Adora loved dancing, and there was no better location to let loose than on a cruise in the middle of Europe. The countries they would be visiting were even more fascinating. Since childhood, Ruben loved history and learned as much as he could about Europe. He was convinced that the trip would ignite this passion and teach him things about the region one cannot learn from without a physical presence. The cruise was to start in Amsterdam, make its way through Germany and France, and end in Switzerland. Adora knew some French and was especially thrilled to learn about the languages of the countries they would be visiting. Her eyes lit up when Ruben told her they would be making a stop in Strasbourg. "Germany's little France!" she proclaimed. Ruben responded with a smile.

A month later, it was time for their flight to Amsterdam. Ruben and Adora had packed all their things the day before and planned to meet Pol and Ruby at Jacksonville International Airport. Once at the airport, the group had a quick lunch and spoke about their dreams for the vacation. Ruby said she hoped to see someone in

"Lederhosen," Pol said he was especially eager to visit the Holocaust Museum, and Adora once again mentioned her admiration for Strasbourg. All Ruben could do was beam from ear to ear. Of course, he was overwhelmed and excited to visit Europe again and impressed Adora with his knowledge of Europe due to his recent deployment to the North Sea. But this was overshadowed by the infatuation he had for Adora. He thought of the Rhine as the perfect opportunity to show her just how much he cared. Ruben knew that this trip was going to be one of a kind. He would do anything to make her happy, and a Rhine cruise was a testament to the deep love he already had for her. As they passed through the boarding gate, they saw the enormous airplane that would take them to Amsterdam. Holding Adora's hand, he looked at her and asked, "Are you ready for a trip of a lifetime?"

Chapter 2:
All Aboard the Viking Tialfi!

On the Plane, Ruben didn't know what to expect. Adora fell asleep on his shoulder while he paged through the Amsterdam travel guide, he bought back in Jacksonville. Pol and Ruby sat behind them, chatting endlessly about their upcoming adventure. Ruben felt a headache arising. Perhaps it was the change in air pressure. He was used to the movements of a ship, but an airplane was a different story. Luckily, Adora remembered to pack in pain tablets, and he took one of them. The pill made him drowsy, and in 30 minutes, he joined Adora in a state of blissful sleep. He was only awakened by the pilot's voice over the intercom. "We are beginning our descent to Amsterdam Airport Schiphol." By now, it was the afternoon, and Amsterdam could be seen clearly as the sun was directly above. During the descent, Pol said his eyes were popping, possibly a complaint he shared with the baby two seats down, that didn't stop crying. Yet, the descent was over as soon as it began, and the group was delighted when the seatbelt sign went off. Ruben didn't understand why so many people jumped up while the plane was still moving. He asked Adora, "Don't they know we're going to the same place?" She didn't reply but nodded in agreement. While they were in the terminal waiting for their bags, they saw a woman who was everything but happy. She was yelling at an employee, complaining about a small tear in her bag, insisting it wasn't there before. The group pointed to her and tried their best not to show the crowd their laughter at her overreaction. Luckily, their bags were just as they had left them in the United States, with their Viking luggage tags—given to them at the time of booking—still firmly attached to the handles.

Just as they walked through the doors labeled "Arrivals," a tall, slender man with blonde hair stood with red Viking lollipops awaiting the arrival of guests. Ruben and the group proudly adorned the Viking stickers attached to their shirts. They were given this in the United States so that the Viking representative could identify them as soon as they walked on Dutch soil. They made their way to the representative, who by this time was labeled "The Lollipop Man" by Ruby. He introduced himself as Luca. Other fellow travelers joined the group, and they soon made their way to a transfer bus. Three other American couples were among them, and Ruben felt a sense of comradery with his fellow travelers. The bus driver put their bags in the trunk and welcomed the excited crowd onto the bus. The driver seemed very proud of his country and was eager to show the Americans the various attractions as they drove to the harbor. The ride lasted about 25 minutes, and all the travelers were keenly invested in what they were being told by Luca and the driver. They all noted that there were bicycles everywhere. "No wonder the Dutch are in such good physical shape, they cycle everywhere!" Adora exclaimed. Once at the harbor, the crew was already awaiting them. Ruben had all their documents in order, as did Pol, leaving them relaxed about the process. The crew quickly took their baggage and transported it to their respective staterooms. Ruben and Pol were given room card keys, and one baggage handler noted, "You're good to go," in a thick Dutch accent. "Bedankt," Ruben replied. He had spent some time learning common Dutch phrases and reluctantly took his first opportunity to exhibit his newly found knowledge. The crew was thrilled with his effort, and he led the group on the gangway. Before climbing aboard, they looked at the vessel. "It's magnificent," Pol exclaimed.

Their vessel, Tialfi, was a riverboat in every respect of the term. However, it is not to be misconstrued with the small, wooden river boats one naturally is inclined to think of. It is much grander than that. Viking—the company that owns the ship—has been in operation since 1997 and has a fleet of 76 ships (Macmillan, 2020). Not only do they offer river cruises, but they have ships all over the world, including those built for ocean travel. Their ships operate in various countries, such as Russia and Egypt, to name only two. The Tialfi is one of their prized vessels and is also referred to as a canal boat. It was launched in 2016, whereafter it began regular cruises on the Rhine. Ruben and his group were hence to travel on a fresh vessel without all the trademarks that threaten smooth travel on an older ship. Pol was correct to call

Tialfi magnificent. The vessel is 443 feet long, has four decks, and has a capacity for 190 passengers in 95 outside cabins (Viking Tialfi Ship Information, n.d.). To Ruben, it seemed like a hotel on the water, even before boarding. The large windows along the length of the ship made it look like a museum of sorts, with the banks of the Rhine as its precious attraction. Given that the Tialfi lies low on the water, the angle of the gangway was something Ruben wasn't used to. In the Navy, he had become accustomed to a gangway pointed to the heavens. This gangway was different. It was completely straight and gave one the impression of stepping over rather than stepping up. A scenario Adora and Ruby were grateful for.

As soon as they entered, Ruben was assured that his choice for a cruise was the correct one. The interior was magnificent. When they entered the reception area, they were met on the main staircase. The side of the staircase was encrusted with marble and gave the appearance that it cost a lot to build this vessel! Adora was drawn to the little shop situated right by the entrance and mentioned that she would love to have a deeper look at the items for sale. Most items were encrusted with symbols glorifying the Tialfi and one's experience with Vikings. She thought it might be a good reminder to take back home once the trip finished. Pol and Ruby looked around and admired the extravagant couches and seating options around the entrance. One side was glass, giving the impression that you were outside. Natural lighting from above made Ruben feel like he never entered a ship in the first place. A crew member invited the group for welcoming drinks and snacks on the Aquavit Terrace at the bow of the ship. He led them up the stairs and pointed to where it was located. Half of the terrace had no roof, and another had a glass roof for when the rain would hinder the trip. Around the deck were tables for groups of four, perfect for Ruben's group. They took their seats and looked at the buildings of Amsterdam. The vessel was docked near the city, making sightseeing from the water possible. "This ship is luxurious!" Adora noted. Ruben held her hand and said that he hoped this trip would be everything she hoped for. She gave him a kiss, but her eyes were drawn to the snacks. When the refreshments were presented, Pol immediately jumped out of his seat and walked to the table to grab a serving plate. The group was hungry and couldn't wait to indulge in Dutch cuisine. Ruby especially enjoyed the Bitterballen and Kroketten, which to her, looked like small meatballs. As she picked this from the buffet, the server explained to her how it was made. "We fill them with a ragout of meat or vegetable and deep-fry it," he said while he directed her towards the mustard it's traditionally eaten with. They were offered champagne, but Ruben thought it might be the wrong choice, given that they had landed a mere hour ago. He chose to have fresh orange juice instead. While eating, the Cruise Director told those seated they had the rest of the day to spend as they wished. Whether they wanted to tour Amsterdam or stay on board to familiarize themselves with the vessel was up to each passenger. The Cruise Director also explained that the passengers will be divided into groups and a local tour guide will be provided for every group.

Adora told Ruben she was tired from their journey thus far and wanted to take a nap. Ruben readily accepted this proposition and told Pol and Ruby they were going to be in their room for a while. Ruben and Adora's veranda were on the same deck as the reception. On the other hand, Pol and Ruby's stateroom were on the top deck. To reach their staterooms, they needed to take the stairs. Ruben took a quick shot of Adora standing next to the modern painting at the top of the stairs. She looked so beautiful that Ruben couldn't help but look at the picture a few times before dropping the camera. The hallway to their stateroom was cozy. It had a light beige carpet with symbols that Ruben had never seen before on any other ship. Moreover, the door was modern but gave the impression of hearkening back to the gilded age of cruise ships. Their veranda stateroom was equally impressive. It had a double bed, two nightstands, a chair, a television, a closet, and two deck chairs resting on their wood-surfaced balcony. Adora mentioned how white the bed sheets were. "It's as if the room was made for us!" she exclaimed. The bathroom was small but functional. It consisted of a toilet, a sink, and a shower, all white. Adora unpacked their clothes while Ruben stood outside with his camera capturing a few shots of the river. They had not yet set sail, but it already felt like the cruise had started.

Pol and Ruby similarly went to their cabin. Their cabin had the same setup as the veranda; however, it lacked the balcony Ruben had paid extra for. "This room is comfortable enough for us," Ruby said. Pol nodded in agreement. The couple wasn't as keen to unpack their luggage just yet. They opted to go for a quick walk around Amsterdam, clearly not feeling as fatigued as Ruben and Adora. As they walked down the stairs to the gangway, they saw a coffee station. "We'll definitely make use of this!" Pol noted. Ruby knew exactly where she wanted to go. Before they left the United States, she did a lot of research on tourist attractions close to the harbor. Two stood out to her: Amsterdam Museum and the Oude Kerk. Fortunately for them, the Tialfi was a short walking distance from both attractions! Pol thought that a walk would do them good after hours of sitting while flying over the Atlantic. Their first stop was the Amsterdam Museum. Ruby loved history and wanted to know everything she could about the Dutch past. The museum was the perfect spot for this. While roaming, they were entranced by the many artifacts scattered throughout the viewing rooms. Pol was especially taken aback by the historical clothing on the mannequins. The decorated clogs delighted the pair. They've read about it, but seeing the wooden shoes was an entirely different experience. Pol wondered how the Dutch could have walked in those heavy shoes. Fortunately, the interactive feature next to the clogs explained that some wore them as shock absorbents while working in the field. "Now it makes sense!" Pol exclaimed.

After a thorough walkthrough, the pair saw a sign for the Mokum Museum Café. They were thirsty and decided to sit down for a cappuccino and a glass of water. Ruby looked at her watch. "We better get going if we want to see the Oude Kerk." Pol went to the bathroom, and soon they were in the picturesque streets of Amsterdam once again. The canals were more beautiful than in pictures, and the couple verbalized a quick appreciation for Ruben, who suggested the trip in the first place. Because they had learned about Amsterdam at the museum, they had a new appreciation for all the sights they saw. The Oude Kerk was even discussed there, making the anticipation to see it even more sublime. Yet, on their way there, they walked through the Red-Light District. The Netherlands is quite progressive, and prostitution has been legal since 2000. Many in this line of work use the Red-Light District as their mode of operation. The pair were astonished by how modern and respectful it seemed. Back in the States, they thought of prostitution as something that happens discreetly. Here, workers stand in windows with no sense of shame or anxiety about police involvement. "What a place for a church!" Paul laughingly said. Ruby was somewhat uncomfortable, but once they entered the doors of the majestic Oude Kerk, this uneasiness was forgotten. It dates from the 14th century, and medieval architecture can clearly be seen in every nook and cranny of the building. Similarly, it had a high tower that the pair could climb to the top of. Pol had a fear of heights but was comforted by a fellow tourist. "If the tower has stood for 800 years, I doubt it's going to crumble now!" The climb was worth it. They saw a great deal of Amsterdam from a bird's eye view. Ruby tried to look for the Tialfi, wondering what Ruben and Adora were up to.

Back on board, Ruben and Adora were fast asleep, enjoying a desperately needed nap. Because they were going to see Amsterdam tomorrow, they figured it would be okay to use their boarding day to rest. Even so, earlier on the terrace, the group was told a drill was going to happen that evening before dinner. Ruben knew all about the muster drill due to his years of experience in the Navy. The others in the group? Not so much. Talking about a drill made Adora anxious. She remembered the unfortunate figures she saw when watching Titanic, jumping for their lives. However, it was necessary. Ruben explained the basics, but the group was still required to attend the drill in the sun deck. By now, Pol and Ruby were back and knocked on Ruben and Adora's room. Luckily, they were awake, showered, and dressed. "Let's go to the drill," Ruben told them. They climbed to the sun deck, ready to learn about their required actions during an emergency. "You jump if I jump?" Adora quoted Rose in Titanic. The group snickered at her analogy. "Don't be silly, this ship won't take two hours to sink!" Ruben replied. The snicker then turned to laughter that continued while awaiting instructions. They were given information in case of emergency and a member of the crew showed them how to put on their orange life jackets. Adora had trouble with this. So, Ruben showed her how to attach it and tied it for her affectionately. "You look so cute in your orange attire," he told her with a smile. Pol and Ruby had no trouble and were hoping it would finish quickly because they were famished.

After 30 minutes, the drill was over, and the group took their seats for dinner. The tables aren't up for reservation, and the group jumped up to pick a corner table that seemed more private. As soon as they sat, the waiter walked up to the table. He had black hair and introduced himself as Willem. He first asked the group if they had any allergies; none of them had. Then he explained the process of the menu. Dinner is three courses, and each person can choose what they want for each course. White or red wine or both is offered for dinner. Additionally, drinks are to be topped up whenever they wish, alcohol and non-alcoholic alike. "We have an open bar!" Pol exclaimed. Ruben—not a fan of alcohol—opted for a Coke light and the rest of the group had champagne. Together they decided to have a traditional Dutch experience on their first night on board. "From tomorrow, we can each eat what we want," Adora claimed. They started with soup: *Groentensoep met balletjes*. Willem told them it was a vegetable soup with small meatballs. Ruben enjoyed this, but Pol was not a fan. He only ate half, and the group made jokes about his love for bland cuisine! "Don't eat too much," Ruben interrupted, "We still have two more courses to go." Thereafter they had *slavinken* with little boiled potatoes. This consisted of meat wrapped in bacon. The entire group loved this meal. "Anything with bacon is my favorite," Adora said to Ruben with a shy smile. He looked at her and fell more in love with her every second. For dessert, they had *vanilla vla*. To them, it looked like cream, but once they took a bite they were mesmerized by its soft texture. It seemed to melt into one's mouth with every bite. Ruben addressed the table, "I just wanted to say thank you for joining me on this trip, guys." "No, thank you for coming up with the idea!" Ruby chipped in. After dinner, they took a stroll on deck, admiring the night lights of Amsterdam. "We're off to bed," Pol noted a short while later. The couples went their separate ways. "Let's go to the room," Adora told Ruben. As they walked to their stateroom, Ruben held Adora's hand. "What a magical day; I can't wait for what's to come tomorrow," Ruben uttered wearily as the two fell asleep in each other's arms.

Chapter 3:
Day 1—Walking the Streets of Amsterdam

"Amsterdam lives and breathes creativity. One moment you walk into a building from the 17th century, and the next, you find yourself in a hub of creative start-up companies" (Wanders). It is often described as the "New York " of Holland due to its rich history and contemporary evolution as required by modern society. The history of Amsterdam is thousands of years old, having been founded at the end of the 12th century. It was first a fishing village but underwent rapid development from 1585 to 1672, colloquially known as its Golden Age. Amsterdam grew to become a commercial success and started a long journey of urban expansion. This period set the stage for the Amsterdam in existence today, characterized by a series of canals and the presence of *rijtjeshuizen*—attached townhouses—and *woonboten*—houseboats. The late 18th century to early 19th century was a time of turmoil as France occupied the region resulting in many homes being evacuated because of economic recession. Yet, from 1813 onwards, the city recovered, and the advent of the industrial revolution saw an even greater influx of Dutch citizens to the city. Canals were filled in, and housing development spread wider with every passing year. Amsterdam became a financial force to be reckoned with in Europe. Sadly, the city was occupied by Nazi Germany during World War II, thereby facing destruction and extermination of the thriving Jewish population who had settled there. Recovery after the war was tedious, but it has led to a flourishing Amsterdam, which is now the center of the country that has one of the highest-earning populations in the world.

Semblances of these historical periods are scattered throughout the city and prickle the interest of any tourist who visits the region. Even so, Ruben has always been a student of history. One of the reasons he chose the Rhine cruise in the first place was to take advantage of the various European stops the cruise was going to make. He read up on Amsterdam and was ecstatic when he found that he would be seeing the city for himself on the first day. That morning, Ruben woke up and found that Adora was in the shower. He wiped his eyes and looked out the window. For a moment, he couldn't believe he had just enjoyed a much-needed rest on the banks of Amsterdam. "Are you awake?" Adora shouted from the bathroom. "Yes, I am, we should probably go to breakfast soon," Ruben replied. After a shower, Ruben got dressed. He saw that the weather was somewhat cloudy and appreciated Adora's recommendation that he should wear a sweater. Shortly after, they met up with Pol and Ruby in the reception area. "Did you sleep well?" Ruby asked them while looking through items in the little shop next to them. "I feel fresh and ready to tackle Amsterdam!" Ruben replied. The group made their way to the dining room, where a buffet was awaiting them. Each grabbed a plate. Ruben opted to have scrambled eggs, a few slices of cheese, and traditional Dutch bread known as *Hoornse broeder*. It was delicious. He didn't really notice what the others were eating because his mind was occupied with anticipation of the upcoming tour. "Continue eating, I'm just going to give you a short run-down of the tour," a tall Dutch man addressed the dining room. The trip was going to last four hours, whereby passengers had the opportunity to follow him or go on it alone. "Perhaps it's better if we go with the tour guide," Adora said. "I agree; that way, we'll see the sights and learn about its history," Ruby replied.

The group soon finished eating, grabbed their silent boxes from their cabins, and waited for the tour guide in the comfortable seating area adjacent to reception. Back in the United States, Ruben was told about the silent boxes waiting for them on the Tialfi. It looked like headphones that would accompany each passenger as they went sightseeing. The frequency was to be adjusted at the instruction of the tour guide. In the reception area, Pol told the group about what they saw yesterday, explaining that the city center is very close to the harbor and wouldn't require a long walk. Four hours was plenty of time. Once they left the Tialfi, they walked towards their first stop: Koninklik Paleis. However, they needed to walk through the Red-Light District to reach it! Ruben and Adora were fascinated by the abundance of women in the area and listened to Pol and Ruby, who pointed things out to them as they walked along the long line of women standing in the mirrors. Adora blushed. "Are you shy?" Ruben asked Adora with a smile. "No, not at all!" Adora replied as she clasped Ruben's hand tightly to protect her from what she was seeing. Fortunately, they quickly reached the place and followed the tour guide inside. He told them that the first floor was open to the public, but rooms on the other floors were still in use by the royal family on occasion, thus barring visitors from entering. The place was originally built in 1655, naturally housing several famous Dutch royals. The central hall was the first room they entered. This spacious room impressed the group. "Look at the statue!" Adora exclaimed. The tour guide heard her and explained that it was a statue of Atlas holding the heavens on his shoulders. The enormity of this room gave Ruben a sense of reverence for Dutch history and the time it needed to build this phenomenal structure. "The ostentatious chandeliers hanging from the decorated roof were installed by Napoleon," the guide mentioned. Thereafter, they walked to the Throne Room and the Moses Hall. Ruben always had a strong faith, and the floor-to-ceiling paintings depicting the story of the biblical Moses stirred his heart. "It's beautiful to see a Bible story with your own eyes, hey Ruben?" Pol noted.

The next stop was the Joods Historisch Museum. Like the palace, it was in the red-light district. However, by now, the group had grown accustomed to the area and didn't look twice. "So, we're going from a Christian center to a Jewish one," Pol said. The entire group had watched *Schindler's List* and discussed the horrors of the holocaust as they walked towards the attraction that was going to show them the rich history of Jews in Holland. "I've read about Anne Frank," Adora said. The tour guide looked at her and mentioned that Anne Frank was only one of the millions of Jews who have walked the streets of Amsterdam over centuries. "You're about to learn much more!" he said. When they arrived at the four historical synagogues that now constitute the museum, they saw a large yellow star of David. "I think we've arrived!" Ruben exclaimed. "Quiet!" Adora replied as if to show respect for the troubles of the Dutch Jewish community throughout the ages. The first room they entered contained artifacts from the 16th century to the modern day. Who knew they had such deep roots in Amsterdam? Everywhere they looked, they saw paintings of Dutch communities in every sector of society. "Look at this beautiful yarmulke," Ruby beckoned the group. It was white with gold embroidery and subsequently fascinated Ruben. "To think this was worn by someone more than a hundred years ago!" he noted admirably. Eventually, the tour guide led them into a room that detailed the history of the Holocaust. As they entered, he told them that an estimated 75% of Dutch Jews were killed during World War II (The Netherlands, 2023). Adora looked at Ruben with tears in her eyes. "How could this possibly happen?" she uttered in a somber tone. Ruben didn't have words. All he could do was hold her until she felt better. "I think we should go," Ruby said. She could see Adora was getting emotional and felt it best to leave before it would upset her even further.

The group shared a sigh of relief when they left the museum. Of course, the dark history of the region is important to witness. But for the sake of enjoying the trip, they were forced to put it in the back of their minds. "Let's do something fun now!" Pol said. The tour guide led the group to an area closer to the harbor where further attractions could be visited. Walking next to the canal, Ruben saw a small canal boat flow past. The passengers seemed to laugh about something that was just said. "I don't think we need to go on one of these, we've already got our sea legs!" Ruben said. The group agreed with his observation and followed the tour guide. Adora was acutely invested in a little shop that had a wide range of Dutch souvenirs. She found herself standing still, especially appreciating the array of napkins with Dutch phrases woven into the fabric. "Let's get going, we don't want to fall behind," Ruby admonished. "Next stop is the flower market!" the tour guide said over Ruben's headphones. Ruben knew that Adora loved flowers and was secretly planning to buy her a beautiful rose once there. Given that the flower market is in Amsterdam, it's expectantly floating on water! It has been in business since 1862 and has become a beacon of pride for the Amsterdam community. It was advertised by their tour guide as one of the most colorful areas in the city, a much-needed departure from the gloomy experience they had just had. When they entered, they were mesmerized. The wall overlooking the river was built of glass. "It's almost like we're on the Tialfi again!" Ruby said. Fortunately, the mood of the group was lifted, and they could enjoy the beautiful sights they saw. It seemed like every flower under the sun had a home here. Ruben noted the tulips and geraniums first. He beckoned Adora to view them with him. "Which one do you like?" he asked. Her eyes were drawn to pink geraniums. "Look how beautiful these are!" Although Ruben had made his mind up about buying Adora a red rose, she liked these more. Close to the geraniums, an old woman was standing with an apron that looked like it had been worn many times before. In a strong Dutch accent, she quoted the popular saying, "Never trust a man or a woman who is not passionately devoted to geraniums!" (Nichols & Dicks, 2009, p. 106). Ruben was convinced. When Adora looked away, he bought a few and presented them to her with a shy expression on his face. Adora was delighted and gave him a kiss on the cheek. Ruben blushed. "It seems like the tour guide wants us to meet up with him at the entrance," Pol mentioned to the group. "Maybe it's lunchtime," Ruby noted with a glimmer of hope. By now, they were all tired of walking and could do with a refreshment. The tour guide explained that anyone could grab a bite to eat from one of the varieties of restaurants close to the market. He ended off with a cautionary, "Don't wander too far off!"

Looking around the harbor for a place to eat, they quickly stumbled on Loetje aan 't Ij. The structure was magnificent. All around the restaurant were high curved pillars supposedly holding up the elevated roof. Ruben thought that it looked like a museum on water! They were convinced that this was the place to eat. Once they entered, they saw a huge LED ceiling giving the impression that one was underwater. The group found a seat right on the edge of the balcony overlooking the river. When the menu came, they were all nervous as it was only in Dutch! They were hoping the waiter spoke English for translation purposes. Luckily, he did. "What would you recommend?" Ruben asked. "I would suggest the *focaccia met gerookte salm*—flatbread with salmon—or *focaccia met geitenkaas*—flatbread with goat's cheese." Ruben and Pol took the first, and Ruby and Adora opted for the second. On this day, Ruben wanted to join the group in drinking alcohol and enjoying a glass of white wine with lunch. The salmon was delicious. He shared the meal with Adora and relished the goat's cheese. "I wonder what time we're expected back on the Tialfi?" Pol asked. Ruby answered, "Probably sooner than later, my feet are killing me!" The group laughed at her response. A laugh that could only mean, "We're in Amsterdam once, forget about your feet!" When lunch was finished, they sat for a while, watching the happenings on the water. Ruben felt tired but was eager to explore a bit more. The tour guide was waiting close to the restaurant when the group left. He instructed the group that their last stop would be the museum quarter: A series of four museums all situated close to each other. They first went to the Rijksmuseum. The museum has over one million objects that detail the history of the Netherlands. Pol was enchanted with over 2000 paintings from various historical periods. "Look at this one's hat," he said as he pointed to the famous painting of The Milkmaid. It was painted in the 1650s and was bought on auction for $40 million in 2004!

After walking around for a while, the tour guide led them to the Van Gogh Museum next door. "Isn't he the one who cut off his own ear?" Adora asked. The group dampened their smirks, not wanting to offend the high regard other tourists supposedly had for the famous painter. Ruben remembered Van Gogh paintings he had seen online but seeing them in person was something else. Specifically, when he saw Van Gogh's self-portrait from 1889. The expression in his eyes seemed somewhat dismal, and he couldn't help but feel sorry for the painter, who, by all accounts, suffered from mental health challenges. "Look! There's the "Wheatfield with Crows," Adora said. Ruben took her hand and walked through the museum, talking about why they thought Van Gogh was this influential. Next, the group was invited to the Stedelijk Museum, which showcases modern art. From the old to the new. Pol and Ruby did not look as interested in these. Modern art was quite different from the literal paintings by the former and seemed to lack the depth of the artwork they had just seen. Nevertheless, the group remained in awe of the various types of art. Roaming through the museum, Ruben felt fatigued. His mind was overwhelmed by all the activities of the day, and he looked forward to boarding the Tialfi again. "I think we can go now," he told the group. They all nodded in agreement. After a day of walking, their staterooms sounded like heaven. Ruben made sure to thank and tipped the tour guide as they arrived at the gangway and entered the vessel. Once inside, both couples went to their staterooms. "Did you enjoy it?" Ruben asked Adora as he put his jacket in the cupboard. "It was magical," Adora replied with a smile. As soon as they laid their heads on the cushions, they fell asleep. A while later, it was time for dinner. They were now accustomed to how the dinner process worked on the Tialfi. Rather than sharing their menu choices, each member of the group chose a different meal. Ruben's main course was fish with vegetables on the side. The conversation around the table centered on the attractions they saw that day. "Can you believe we actually saw Amsterdam?" Adora said, as if for a moment still in wonder that they were actually in Europe. Ruben put his hand on her thigh and knew he had made the right decision of bringing her on this trip. That night Ruben and Adora slept peacefully, holding hands, awaiting the new adventure that was going to be Kinderdijk.

Chapter 4:
Day 2—The Windmills of Kinderdijk

"Love is that to life, what wind is to a windmill" (Shamz, 2021). Simply put, wind gives meaning to a windmill, just as love gives meaning to life. This quote perfectly sums up the objective Ruben had for the trip. Just as Adora gave greater meaning to his life that was to be cultivated on this trip, the windmills of Kinderdijk only prove useful when stimulated by wind. This image was clear in Ruben's mind when the group visited Kinderdijk. The nineteen windmills in Kinderdijk are a far cry from the more than 1,200 windmills in the Netherlands. However, these particular windmills played a crucial role in managing flooding in the region for hundreds of years. Windmills are usually used to generate water from the ground, but those in Kinderdijk are utilized to keep water out. The idea for their construction can be dated back to 1277 when Count Floris V—the ruler of medieval Holland—grew tired of the constant complaints by lords and nobles regarding flooding in the municipality of Molenlanden. He ordered the establishment of the Overwaard and Nederwaard water boards that would oversee a viable solution to the problem. The boards discussed ways in which water could be kept out of the region and decided upon a system of windmills, dikes, and other various construction efforts to drain the land

and transfer excess water to the river. The windmills subsequently became an integral part of the massive water management system. At the time, they weren't labeled, but the name Kinderdijk—Dutch for "Child's Dike"—can be traced back to around 1421. The story goes that the windmills saved a baby and a cat floating in a cradle as the floodwaters subsided. Today, windmills are considered retired due to the advent of modern water pipes, yet they can be brought into action whenever needed. A prominent case when this was done was during World War II when there was an acute shortage in the supply of diesel. Since 1997, the windmills have been listed as a world heritage site because it is regarded as structures that broadcast "human ingenuity and fortitude over nearly a millennium" (5 things you didn't know about the windmills at Kinderdijk, 2019). It is truly a sight to see and was about to be enjoyed thoroughly by Ruben and his group.

When Ruben and Adora woke up, they could see a windmill in the distance. "Come look at this!" Ruben shouted as he ran to the balcony. Adora was quick to follow him and leaned over the railing for a better view. "There's another one!" she yelled with enthusiasm. From afar, they looked huge, and the two were imagining what it was going to look like once they disembarked. Pol and Ruby were already in the dining room and were feasting on scrambled eggs and bacon when they first got a glimpse of the windmills. "Now, this is what you call historical Holland," Pol noted. Ruben and Adora arrived and took a seat at the table. "Could you get me some of those waffles at the far end of the buffet table?" Adora asked Ruben. He got up and dished a big one for the two to share. After a quick discussion about the prospective activities of the day, the Cruise Director entered the room. "We'll be disembarking soon, make sure to wear a jersey, it's a bit chilly in the flood region!" he remarked with a wink. The group scurried to their staterooms to get jerseys. Waiting in the reception area were Pol and Ruby. Ruben and Adora were taking a while, leaving Ruby nervous that they would miss the group of tourists who were already disembarking. Fortunately, they made it in the nick of time and were the last to leave the Tialfi. "First stop, the visitor center!" the tour guide said through their headphones. The group could see the visitor center from where they were standing. "Not as much walking today," Ruby mentioned with a sigh of relief. The center looked immaculately taken care of. The walls were made from glass and seemed even more impressive once entered. Once inside, Ruben looked up and saw a panoramic roof, pointing it out to his fellow tourists. Moreover, there was a souvenir shop and a cozy café, which Adora had already insisted upon going to once they got the chance. On the walls, there were all kinds of photos and paintings of the windmills and a large map that showed the layout of the area. "Looks like we're going to the Wisboom pumping station first," Pol uttered quietly as if he was talking to himself. Nevertheless, the group heard him and followed the tour guide to their first attraction.

The Wisboom pumping station was built in 1868 and still has all the fittings of an authentic Victorian structure: old-fashioned orange bricks and small half-circular windows. Since its decommissioning in 1996, the building now houses the start of one's Kinderdijk journey. Scattered throughout the facility are viewing boxes that allow tourists to take a peek at what the area looked like centuries ago. Ruben—the history buff that he is—made sure to look into each one he could find. At the center of the facility is a table-top replica of the region from a birds-eye view. On this replica were a few miniature windmills scattered about. "You can give it a go," the tour guide said, looking at Adora. Adora felt quite embarrassed as many other tourists now looked at her. She started spinning the wheel. "Spin faster! You don't want the area to flood," Ruben boldly said. Pol and Ruby stood back, seemingly anxious if Adora was going to let Kinderdijk down. Luckily, she was successful and didn't cause any flooding. "Well done! You saved Holland," the tour guide said as the spectators roared with laughter. Adora's slight blush made Ruben fall in love with her more. "Come here," he said as he took her in his arms and gave her a quick kiss on her forehead. All around the interior walls were hand-painted artwork celebrating the history of Kinderdijk. Ruby spent most of her time pondering about the craftsmanship needed to create them "Can you imagine how long it took them to paint these? It's so detailed." Once in the engine room of the facility, the group met the host, who was standing in the corner, supposedly waiting to tell them about the functioning of the facility in its heyday. He told all those present that after the windmills were powered by steam engines, the facility pumped out 425,000 liters per minute, only to double in capacity when Kinderdijk switched to electrically powered pumps in 1924 (Wisboom Pumping Station, n.d.). "It stinks like grease in here," Adora whispered quietly in Ruben's ear. Ruben agreed but went on listening to the host so as to show his deep admiration for the host's vast knowledge of the topic. It looked like Ruby told the same to Pol, and the two men gave each other a sneaky look of acknowledgment. That being said, Ruben and Pol were similarly relieved when they breathed the fresh air as they left Wisboom and walked towards De Fabriek Secondary Pumping station.

De Fabriek was right next door and was by no means as impressive as Wisboom. This is done by design. De Fabriek is predominantly an area where tourists can sit and watch a video explaining the history and functioning of the windmills. After the group had watched the video, a man arrived and stood behind a table in front. He expanded on what was just mentioned in the short video and asked whether anyone had questions. Throughout his speech, Ruben could see Adora's attention span getting the better of her. In fact, Ruben wanted to go outside as well. They did the next best thing; Ruben whipped out his camera and took a few shots of the scene. His favorite one was of Adora giving a confident pose with the instructor looking serious in the background. Ruby and Pol were sitting a few feet away from them and snickered at the supposed bravado Ruben displayed while everyone else was listening quietly. However, this was by no means disrespectful. The instructor welcomed the group to take pictures, but many felt uncomfortable doing so while he was speaking. Yet, Ruben figured that taking pictures might cheer Adora up and put them in a mood that would prove helpful for further exploration. He made the right call. After De Fabriek, they were to visit two of the actual windmills that had been converted into museums. When they left, Ruben exclaimed, "Let's go see these structures we've been hearing about the whole morning up close!" The group didn't have to respond to show that they shared in his excitement. The speed at which they walked was enough proof for Ruben. First, they went to the Blokweer Museum mill. Originally built in 1630, it was renovated in the early 20th century after a devastating fire. The entire mill is decorated exactly the way it was in the 1950s. "It feels like we're going back in time," Adora told the group. Inside, every piece of furniture was antique, and everything seemed so small. Ruben was especially surprised at the tight positioning of a child's bed. "I would get too claustrophobic," Pol remarked. One can imagine the group's amazement when one of the millers walked out. It was an elderly man in traditional clothes; he was even wearing the wooden clogs the group had seen in Amsterdam the day before. "Oh, so that's how it looks on a person," Adora told Ruben as he nodded in agreement. Outside were a few goats, which only added to the historic atmosphere. "You look so beautiful, stand next to the entrance, and I'll take a quick picture," Ruben told Adora. With her arm resting on the bricks dating back from the 17th century, Ruben made up his mind that this was the woman he wanted to marry.

"Next stop, the Nederwaard mill!" the tour guide shouted. Although this mill was originally built a century later than Blokweer, it looked like it was older. Perhaps this is because it doesn't contain much furniture, nor was it burnt down like the former. Before entering, the group looked up and saw the massive sails that made a relatively loud noise as they fought with the wind. "I wouldn't even be able to fall asleep with all that creaking," Ruben heard one of the other tourists mention to a friend. The tour guide soon gave some historical context. "In this mill lived a man with his wife, together with their 13 children." Adora raised her eyebrows and looked at the group with shock. "13 children? We should be glad that we're living in the 21st century!" Pol remarked. The stone walls gave the building an eerie feeling once inside. Some might be prompted to think of a medieval dungeon. Yet, the natural lighting from the windows assures you that you're safe. Not only that, but the stairs were also extremely steep. Ruby opted out of going to the second floor for fear of falling, but Ruben and Adora summoned the courage to go upstairs. There was not much to be seen, but the view was remarkable. From the window, they could view the entire landscape.

Additionally, they were alone, which allowed for some much-needed privacy. "Would you live with me in this mill?" Ruben asked. "I'll live anywhere with you." Her reply brought Ruben great comfort and satisfaction. "What's taking Ruben and Adora so long?" Ruby asked Pol, knowing full well he didn't need to answer. Pol looked at her with a cheeky expression. They both knew what they were thinking. "Let them have some alone time, we're in the continent of love," came the reply. After a few moments, Ruben climbed down the steep stairs. He made sure to stand his ground when Adora descended. Of course, he wanted to be her knight in shining armor should she slip. Fortunately, she didn't need saving on this particular day. "I'm hungry, let's go to the café we saw at the visitors center," Adora proposed. The group slowly made their way back to where they started their Kinderdijk journey. Shortly after lunch, it was time to board the Tialfi once again. The vessel needed to set sail if they were going to reach Cologne by the evening! Ruben and Adora spent the rest of the day sipping cocktails on the terrace overlooking the river. When the ships departed, Adora waved towards the shoreline, giving one the impression that the windmills were not only physical structures but had unique personalities. "Goodbye Kinderdijk!" Adora shouted. "We'll be back," Ruben replied.

Chapter 5:

Day 3—Exploring Cologne

That evening, Ruben and the group ate dinner in the dining room. Ruben was munching away on his steak while Adora chose to have something lighter. While they were in the midst of a conversation, an announcement rang in their ears: "We are now nearing Cologne, welcome to Germany!" Pol, still chewing, sprung up and ran out of the room to be the first to catch a glimpse of a new country without the hindrance of a glass window. It was as though he wanted to smell the German air and beckoned the others to join him. By now, it was dark, and the lights of the city shined bright on the Tialfi. "Look at the cathedral!" Adora yelled. "Stand for a photo with the backdrop of Cologne, we'll want to remember this," Ruben said as he ran back into the dining room to grab his camera. "Pol and Ruby, stand in front of the railing, I want to get a good backdrop," Ruben instructed. After a quick shot was snapped, Ruby urged Ruben to stand for a photo, "You're always the one behind the camera, and it's about time you modeled for us!" Adora smiled and looked at Ruben's pose with great affection. She quickly took a spot next to him and put her arms around his waist for a "Cologne couple's" photo, as Ruby labeled it. The group made their way back to their table and continued eating. Ruben's attention was constantly drawn to the attractions he could see from the full-length windows. "After having seen those lights, I hope I'll be able to sleep tonight," Pol noted. Ruben assured the group that tomorrow would be memorable, and it was best to get enough sleep-in order to enjoy the sightseeing in a few hours. After dinner, they walked back to their respective staterooms. Ruben and Adora spent some time on the balcony, sipping on their Lattés that Adora had made for them in the coffee station. "Let's get to bed, tomorrow is going to be a busy day," Ruben said, before closing the sliding door. Ruben was right. Cologne is an enormous city, and they would need to be in top shape to appreciate the richness of its history.

Cologne—known as Köln in German—is currently the fourth largest city in the country. Moreover, it's one of the oldest in Europe, with strong Roman roots dating back to the dawn of Western civilization. The earliest mention of the city dates back to 50 AD when the region was named Colonia. In ancient times, Cologne was the seat for the governor of Lower Germany. But in the year 785, Cologne became a religious hotspot because Charlemagne made it an archbishopric for the Catholic Church. With time, the appointed archbishops grew in power and ultimately became electoral princes in the 12th century. More than 100 years later, the population was uneasy with this arrangement and revolted, securing Cologne as a free city in 1288. Given that Cologne is situated next to the Rhine, trade funded economic growth and instigated a mass movement of people toward the region for centuries, specifically in the 19th century. The Industrial Revolution introduced railways and steam power that subsequently molded Cologne into a real powerhouse until the tragedy of war reached its borders. The First World War did not prove that destructive for the region, but World War Two hit Cologne especially hard. The city suffered through 262 air raids, resulting in 90% of the inner city being demolished (Wedia, n.d.). Even so, millions of people were evacuated, and previously busy neighborhoods became nothing less than ghost towns. The destruction was so great that Cologne was known as "The world's greatest heap of rubble" around the world in 1945. Fortunately, historical structures were stronger than the devastating face of war, and many can still be seen today. Pride in their history pushed the city's management to promote restoration efforts that lasted until the 1990s; 50 years after the war ended! In recent years, Cologne has become a hub for tourists due to its many historical sights and the perception of Cologne residents as the friendliest in the nation. Ruben's group was soon to experience this city first-hand.

Before disembarking the Tialfi the following day, Ruben and his companions discussed the upcoming trip over breakfast. "Don't you just feel for the tour guide? They must choose a handful of attractions that make up this enormous city," Pol mentioned. Ruben agreed. How could they possibly know what to show the tourists in the timespan of a day? Luckily, their tour guide knew exactly where to take them. Cologne boasts the tallest cathedral in Europe and is a must-see for all those who visit the city. "Obviously, we have to visit that first!" Adora said with enthusiasm. Just as the words exited their lips, the Cruise Director entered the dining room and gave a short rundown of the day's trip. The first stop is the cathedral, followed by a walkthrough of the city, a stop at the famous Cologne Bridge, and ending with a visit to the NS Documentation Centre. "Sounds like a full day, eat up, I'll meet you guys on the docks," Ruben said as he pulled out Adora's chair. After gathering their belongings and earpieces, they disembarked the ship, and met up with Pol and Ruby, who were waiting next to a bus. The tour guide told them that they would not be walking to the cathedral because it's quite a distance that would undoubtedly leave the tourists exhausted if they went on foot. "Perfect," Ruby said with a cheeky smile. "All aboard!" the tour guide yelled excitedly while he welcomed each person on the bus. Ruben and Adora found a seat near the back where there seemed to be a semblance of privacy. She took his hand and held it tight until they reached the cathedral. As they moved closer to the building, Ruben pointed out the two towers, which reached higher than any other building in the vicinity. "Can you believe this thing has been standing for centuries," Adora said as she tightened her grip on his hand.

Other than being immense, the gray exterior of the cathedral leaves many tourists wondering why this structure is so famous. To Adora, it even looked dirty and needed a wash. Yet, the tour guide explained, "Remember, the cathedral is centuries old and was built with a sandstone material that interacts with sulphuric rain, thereby giving it its tone." Ruben urged her to focus on the historical significance and put the dirty texture out of her mind. She quickly came around and gasped when they entered. It was nothing like they'd ever seen. The aisle was never-ending, with an immeasurable number of pews all pointed towards a magnificent altar. The thick pillars scattered throughout the building made the group feel safe. "Although this building is so old, I feel safer here than in my office at work," Pol mentioned. Perhaps it was the many paintings of Christian figures on the windows. Ruby was intrigued by one stained glass window that showed the baby Jesus in his mother's arms. "Some of these dates back to the 14th century," the tour guide mentioned over their earpieces. "When was this cathedral built?" a tourist asked. Motivated by their interest, the tour guide quickly gave a short history of the building. "The area on which the cathedral is built has been a church since the 4th century, but construction of our current location began in 1248 only to be completed in 1880." "Today, no one would wait 400 years for something to be built!" Pol exclaimed to the amusement of other tourists. The tour guide led them to a section behind the high altar, known as the shrine of the Three Wise Men. The gold-encrusted treasure chest is believed to hold the remains of the Three Wise Men, who were present at the birth of Jesus. Ruben was fascinated by this. He imagined that this was the closest he'd ever gotten to the life of the Messiah. "Adora, this has outlived everything that mankind has experienced for two thousand years," Ruben whispered to her. The beautiful artwork that scattered the floor made Ruben check the under soles of his shoes! He surely did not want to ruin the years of effort put into construction. The tour guide instructed the group that they were welcome to go up the tower if taking 533 steps did not bother them! After some contemplation, Ruben was convinced it was worth it. They're only in Cologne once. Pol and Ruby opted to stay behind. "Let's go, Adora," Ruben said in an attempt to convince himself that a workout session was worth it. After some deep breaths, they tackled the stairs and were surprised to find it easier than they had thought. Not only did Ruben and Adora see a panoramic view of Cologne when they reached the top, but they passed the cathedral's bell—called "Fat Peter"—which is the biggest of its kind in Europe. Nevertheless, once they descended, they had to catch their breath in one of the pews with Pol and Ruby by their side. "Off to the bridge!" the tour guide's voice sounded over Ruben's earpiece.

Ruben's legs were quite sore after the hundreds of steps he and Adora had just taken. However, their walk through the city toward the Hohenzollern Bridge was a short one. The tour guide instructed: "For the lovebirds, make sure to buy a padlock at a store I'll point out to you." Ruben winked at Adora. A few moments later, the shop was visible, and Ruben bought a padlock with a key:

a red one with a big white hook. After taking a picture of Adora outside of the shop, Ruby beckoned the couple to follow the tour guide. "We don't want to get lost in Cologne!" she advised. From a distance, the bridge did not look impressive. Yet, once they arrived and saw thousands of locks attached to its railings, Ruben knew why the tour guide urged a purchase. "It is said that if you attach your padlock to this railing, your love will strengthen. But make sure to throw the key in the Rhine! That way, your love will last forever," the tour guide mentioned. Adora supposedly felt intimidated by the notion and funnily mentioned, "Don't we have an extra key in case…" "In case what?" Ruben responded with big eyes and a melodramatic facial expression. Both laughed and knew that their love would last a lifetime. Pol and Ruby stepped away so as to give the lovebirds some space. It was here that Ruben said three words that changed the nature of their relationship forever: "I love you." Adora was taken aback by his gesture and replied in kind. A kiss followed the verbalization of their deepest feelings and set the stage for their promised commitment on the bridge. "Hold the key," Ruben said as he picked a spot to put their padlock. He found the perfect one. Their padlock's neighbor had *du und ich*—you and I—written on it, and the couple felt safe to attach theirs next to this sweet sentiment. After locking it, Adora threw the key into the river. "Now you're stuck with me forever," Ruben said in a shy tone. Adora didn't reply. She simply closed her eyes and went in for a kiss. Pol and Ruby looked on from a distance, sharing a smile as they witnessed the love shared between two people, they knew were made for each other. Ruben and Adora were so infatuated that, for a moment, Ruben forgot where he was. Adora blushed, and Ruben finally felt at peace, knowing his love was definitely reciprocal. Sadly, they couldn't stay there the entire day. "We should probably get back to the bus."

The love and admiration they felt soon turned into one of sadness when the bus arrived at their next stop: The NS-Documentation Centre. The group had seen some sights related to the holocaust, but this one was different as it served as the headquarters for the Gestapo—the political police of Nazi Germany—during the darkest time in the history of Germany. The building was beautiful from the outside but once entered, the group felt a sense of horror and reverence for the dead. The walls are left just as they were during the 1930s and 1940s, giving one the impression that you are taking a time machine back to the era. Scattered across the walls are newspaper articles, pictures of holocaust victims, and interactive features allowing one to hear the stories of victims. One picture garnered a strong response from Adora. It was a three-tier photograph of a Jewish woman who was imprisoned. "You can see the fear on this poor woman's face," she said as she wiped a tear from her cheek. Similarly, Pol looked teary-eyed while listening to a story told by a survivor on one of the screens. "This man lost his entire family, I can't even imagine the pain he must have felt," he said while walking towards the holding cells. In the center are 10 cells where many people were tortured and killed. Ruben was touched by the many drawings arched in the walls of these cells; their creators murdered by the Nazis. Moreover, the courtyard of the building was a sight of countless executions and stirred anger in Ruben. He was at a loss for words. He felt angry at the perpetrators while at the same time feeling profound heartache for all those who suffered. "This is just so sad," he uttered to himself. The one good thing that came from this visit was the gratitude Ruben expressed for his life and freedoms. Here, he was in Europe with the love of his life, not knowing if this day could be his last as well. "Never take a single day for granted," he told the group as they exited the facility.

It was time to board the Tialfi, majestically waiting for them in the harbor. On their bus trip back to the vessel, Ruben and Adora spoke about their padlock. "I wonder if we're going to sail over it this evening," she mentioned to Ruben with her hand resting on his knee. Ruben thought of their last attraction, still in the midst of agony about the holocaust. Pol and Ruby similarly seemed touched by the visit and looked like they needed a long nap to invigorate their spirits. The bus soon stopped near the ship, and they walked onto the gangway into the Tialfi. Although this had only been their residence for a few days, it started to feel like home. A buffet-style refreshment station was waiting for them in the dining room, and the group made a quick visit before retiring to their staterooms. Pol, still unnerved about the NS documentation center, was eerily quiet. Ruby noted that he just looked out of the window while chewing his food thoughtlessly. "I think it's time to go to the room," she said to him after finishing her Coca-Cola. "We'll see you at dinner," Ruben mentioned while they were getting up from their seats. Ruben and Adora took a much-needed nap, opting to have room service that evening. All the activities of the day made them tired, and they wanted some alone time. They spent hours on the balcony, admiring the views in silence. "I wonder what we can expect in Koblenz," Ruben noted as the two drifted off to sleep with the lights of Cologne dimming as the vessel traversed the Rhine.

Chapter 6:

Day 4— German Unity in Koblenz

The Tialfi arrived in Koblenz in the early morning hours while Ruben and Adora were still asleep. Luckily, the couple woke up in time to see the promontory that separates the Rhine from the Mosel River. At the center of the structural separation—known in the region as the "German Corner"—stood an enormous statue of a man on his horse. "That's Emperor William I of Prussia!" Ruben shouted as he ran to the balcony to get a closer look. He had learned about William I in school and seemed to remember everything about this figure's life when confronted with his statue. He enthusiastically told Adora about this man. "Although William only ruled for 10 years, he was responsible for the unification of the nation and was the first to rule the Germany we see today." Adora was intrigued at Ruben's vast knowledge about a person who had lived more than a hundred years ago. He went on, "Did you know he survived at least one assassination attempt and died at the age of 90?" To Adora, it made sense that William would be celebrated on the corner of the nation he supposedly unified. In Pol and Ruby's stateroom, however, there was silence. The two were still fast asleep, only to be awakened when Ruben arrived at their door to invite them for breakfast. "We're in Koblenz! You slept through our arrival,"

Ruben jokingly reprimanded. Pol, still rubbing his sleepy eyes, nodded and said they'll get ready for breakfast. During mealtime, Adora made a few jokes about the couple sleeping through such a big event. Ruby snickered at her comments, and Pol rolled his eyes as Ruben looked on, appreciating Adora's sense of humor. A while later, the Cruise Director made his entrance once again and gave a short rundown of the day's activities. After a quick trip to their staterooms accomplished, the group left the Tialfi, all ready to explore the city that symbolizes unity.

Koblenz is much older than Germany itself. Several artifacts have been found that indicate the region was occupied no later than 1000 BCE. However, it became an established city in 9 BCE after the Romans expanded the empire into the area. As in Cologne, Koblenz was a site under the leadership of archbishops who were appointed by Charlemagne at the same time as the former. During this period, the city grew and became a thriving establishment wherein many rural citizens chose to live. In 1214 Koblenz was chartered and welcomed many immigrants from all over Europe. 600 years later, it was incorporated into Prussia and became the capital of the Prussian Rhine Province. The strategic location of the area made it the perfect spot for an administrative body after World War I, known as the Inter-Allied Control Commission. The commission oversaw the occupation of the Rhineland after Germany was forced to abide by the stipulations outlined in the Treaty of Versailles. Similar to Cologne, World War I devastated the city, and much of its history was lost to bombings and military campaigns. Yet, many of these were restored and now look as they had for hundreds of years. Scattered throughout Koblenz are medieval churches that take one back to a bygone age. Moreover, many citizens take pride in the Ehrenbreitstein Fortress, which stands 387 feet above the Rhine. Ruben and Adora saw this massive building when they awoke that morning. "It almost looks like a prison," Adora noted. In fact, Adora was not wrong. Although it never served as a prison, it was used by the Prussian government to defend Germany in case of conflict. It's a small town full of forts, redoubts, and flèches dating back to the Victorian era. In the evenings, the lights of the fortress shine bright over the river and are akin to a castle one only reads of in fairytales. Many of the sights in Koblenz can be seen from the river, which is possibly why the Cruise Director informed the group that they would be taking a bus seven miles southeast of Koblenz to the Marksburg Castle once they disembarked.

During the bus ride on their way to the castle, Adora was ecstatic. Sure, they'd seen cathedrals and a palace, but this would be their first trip to a medieval castle. Her excitement was not in vain. As the bus drove closer to its destination, Ruben was the first to see the white castle perched high on the hill. Ruby called the group to look at the towers. "Looks like the castle in Cinderella, does it not?" she said with the animation of a little girl. As a child, Adora dreamt of a prince on a white horse whisking her away to his castle. Although Ruben was far from royalty, he took pride in being the first man to make her fairytale dream come true. "We might not be able to live here, but maybe we could stay for the ball," he remarked. Adora smiled. The closer they got to Marksburg, the more impressed the group became with the enormity of the structure. On the bus, their tour guide gave some history of the building. "The castle was built in stages," he said, "the earliest mention of the castle dates back to 1231 when it was owned by the Eppstein family, who were responsible for the basic layout." Ruben looked out of the window, appreciating the lush surroundings. The tour guide continued, "In 1281, the castle was bought by an influential count with subsequent ownership being hereditary until the last one died in 1479." The dates were making Ruby confused. "He already lost me at 1281," she whispered to Pol. Nevertheless, the tour guide went on, "After the period of counts, the castle became a fortress that was aimed at keeping the area safe from the war until 1803, whereafter it was transformed into a prison and a home for injured soldiers." Although Ruby was lost, Ruben was fascinated by the tour guide's knowledge. "I read that the castle was utilized as apartments, am I correct?" Ruben interjected. The tour guide was pleased with Ruben's interest and explained, "That is true; however, the administration of the building was not caring for the structure appropriately, and it was purchased by the German Castles Association in 1900." This explains why Marksburg is still the headquarters of this association, tasked with preserving the many medieval monuments scattered throughout the nation. With the theory taken care of, the group now wanted to enter the castle and see the age-old building for themselves.

Once parked, the group got out and saw the majestic castle up close. "Stand in front of the view, this is an amazing backdrop," Ruben asked Adora as he grabbed his camera from his backpack. The tour guide called the group to the entrance. He explained that they would be walking through four gates. "Now that's security!" Pol noted. The first they entered was the Drawbridge Gate. Today the platform does not rise anymore, but in medieval times, the entrance could be lifted so as to resist any "unwelcome" visitors. The tour guide pointed out the room in which the gatekeeper slept hundreds of years ago. Ruben was intrigued that he was walking into a building that had been lived in for centuries. The next gate was the *Fuchstor*—Fox Gate—which allowed for extra protection if enemies were to pass the first. The group walked through the Arrow Slit Gate next as they walked the stairs upwards. The tour guide stood still for a moment, "Take note of the machicolation above your heads; this small window was used to throw stones or boiling water onto enemies who made it this far!" Adora looked worried for only a second, supposedly wondering whether she should duck for an undesired rock thrown her way! The last gate is known as the Rider's Stairway, which, to the dismay of Adora and Ruby, requires a steep climb. "Why are the floors so uneven? One can barely walk," Ruben asked the tour guide. "This is by no accident or decay; they were specifically built like this so that horses wouldn't slip." Adora was beginning to wonder whether the castle was merely a series of gates to be passed through. Fortunately, this was the last, and they were soon inside the castle.

After walking past the Romanesque Palas, the structure that houses the aforementioned association, the group ended up in the Battery. This area was the center of operations during conflict situations. Ruben imagined hundreds of soldiers running about this area. Leaving no room for imagination, the tour guide pointed out a cannon that was placed there in 1450. Some cannons were larger than others, but in conjunction with each other, they had an approximate aim width that spanned 1000 meters, thereby enabling stationed soldiers to protect the entire width of the Rhine. "What if one of these are pointed to the Tialfi?" Ruby stated to the amusement of the other tourists. "Next stop, the garden." Before reaching the estimated 150 different species of medieval plants and herbs, the group was told to refrain from touching them as some are poisonous. So potent, in fact, that medieval witches were said to use them in concocting potions. Ruben saw plants in colors he didn't think possible, but his eyes were constantly drawn to the Rhine lying regally in the distance. Now, it was time to go inside. First, they climbed a wooden staircase in order to reach the courtyard. Ruben held on to Adora's waists so as to capture her should she fall.

They were now in the wine cellar that was built in the 17th century. The old black barrels left much to desire, especially in the dark tomb-like room they were in. "I'm getting quite claustrophobic," Adora told Ruben while she put her hands under his jacket for a soft hug. "Don't worry, we're almost done here," Ruben reassured her.

The kitchen was a sight to see. "This area was used only by servants as the noble family ate upstairs," the tour guide said. It was constructed in 1435 and still has many utensils that were used by medieval chefs. The room smelled old, but the fake pieces of the meat reminded Ruben that they were indeed in the 21st century. "Look at the dead birds hanging on the wall!" Adora shouted as she grabbed Ruben closer. An animal lover, Adora felt sorry for the poor creatures displayed on hooks. Nonetheless, she refrained from going closer to check if they were real. The tour guide mentioned that the kitchen could be booked for a private supper, a proposition Adora certainly would not accept. "I don't think I'll be able to get anything down if I'm faced with these dead animals around me." That being said, the group enjoyed looking around at the historical artifacts regarding food preparation. It gave them a strong feeling of reverence for those who roamed the earth before them. Moving from the servants' quarters to that of the noble family, the group was quickly welcomed to their bed chamber. The different sets of families slept in this dark wood-paneled room over the centuries. The bed looked somewhat ostentatious due to the red drapes along the four tall posts. The tour guide explained the reasoning behind these: "It was not uncommon for servants to periodically enter the room, and this was the only source of privacy the noble couple had." Believe it or not, there were a few downsides to being noble! Thereafter followed a walkthrough of the great hall where the family enjoyed traveling singers and other forms of entertainment. Ruben was keenly invested in the privy toilet that was reached through a short corridor. It was simply a hole in a wooden seat. "Whoever invented plumbing, I salute you," he told his friends. Pol seemed too afraid to peek down the hole, exclaiming, "We don't want to find a medieval surprise!"

The chapel was not as impressive. Ruben couldn't help but compare it to the enormous cathedral he saw the day before. Yet, the small scale of this prayer room was understandable. The tour guide noted, "Only the family used this room for spiritual purposes," meaning that this was all they needed. It was not clear where the servants went for spiritual counsel, but Ruben was convinced that that chapel was lost to history. "We're going to walk through the Rhine wing now; I would suggest you grab onto a loved one in front of you," the tour guide instructed. Adora and Ruby's eyes widened, and their worry was clear to the men. The reason for this advice became evident when they started walking the stairs. It looked like a dungeon wherein one could quickly feel acutely confined. However, the short wing was worth the short feeling of anxiety as it brought them to the

"Gimbel Collection." This collection consists of 12 mannequins that are dressed in armor from the different periods of Markburg's long life. Moreover, there was a small glass cabinet that held artifacts found throughout the castle. Pol recognized the natural sequence of the armor. It seemed like the armory started off by leaving some room for comfortable movement, and ended off being wholly constrictive, covered in heavy iron. Even the shoes were made from iron. "If I were to wear one of these, I'd pick number one," Ruben pointed to a mannequin wearing a short skirt. The group burst out in laughter. Adora replied with a wink, "That will be a treat." Rather bashfully, Ruben walked over to the glass cabinet. Their laughs turned to looks of concern when they entered the torture exhibition shortly after.

The tour guide informed the group that prisoners of war were sent to this room when they were to be questioned. The rocky walls made the room feel threatening in itself. Adora made sure to stay close to Ruben as her source of protection from what they were witnessing. "This is the rack," the tour guide said as he pointed to a long wooden table. "A prisoner's arms and legs were first tied to the edges and were then pulled in opposite directions slowly, ultimately pulling their limbs out of their sockets." Ruben couldn't even imagine the pain the respective prisoners went through. Looking across the room, Ruben noticed a small metallic feature. The tour guide, seeing Ruben's wandering eyes, introduced him to this torture mechanism. "This is the thumb screw; the prisoner's thumbs were put into these two holes and tightened until it protruded through their nails." "Give it a go," Pol said with a cheeky smile. Ruben pretended to place his thumbs in the mechanism and pulled it out right before he got nervous. Adora seemed irked at this gesture. "It was just a joke," Ruben uttered with an air kiss. The blacksmith room was their last stop. It's preserved to look exactly as it had in medieval times, with the bronze tools used during that period scattered all around the room. By now, Ruben and the group were feeling tired and much relieved to be boarding the bus once again. The tour guide escorted everyone out of the castle and assisted them onto the vehicle. "I don't think Cinderella had a torture room in her palace," Adora jokingly said to Ruben as they took their seats. "Perhaps that's where she locked up her evil stepsister," he replied. The drive back to Tialfi was quiet. Pol closed his eyes, something Ruben noticed a lot of passengers do. It was time to board the Tialfi and relax. Once on board, the group had lunch on the terrace and went to their staterooms after. "Let's go sit on the balcony," Adora suggested once inside. That evening, the couple sat on the deck looking at the abundance of historical structures standing graciously on the shore. Their lights illuminated the region and proved to be the perfect backdrop for a magical night.

Chapter 7:
Day 5— "I Lost My Heart in Heidelberg"

"I lost my heart in Heidelberg for all time, on a balmy summer night" (Hall, 1932). These are the words in Henry Hall's famous song about flourishing love in the picturesque German city of Heidelberg. Once Ruben knew that their trip would include this city, he sent Adora a link to the song, and it subsequently became one of her favorites. Ruben viewed Heidelberg as the city where their trip would culminate into everything he desired. In fact, the importance he gave to Heidelberg was unnecessary in that their relationship blossomed in Amsterdam! Yet, he was not wrong in expecting it to evolve into something more. Listening to the song back in the United States made the group especially eager to visit the city. "There should be a reason they wrote a song about it," Adora once remarked. On the morning of their trip to Heidelberg, Ruben, and Adora awakened early. Seemingly overjoyed at the prospect of touring the city, Pol and Ruby were the first to wait in the dining room. "Look who beat us this morning!" Ruben said as he walked closer to them. It was probably the first and last day of this occurring, but Pol was proud that, for once, they woke up earlier than their friends. For breakfast, Ruben had scrambled eggs, and Adora had some toast. Pol and Ruby enjoyed egg and bacon on freshly baked bread. The Cruise Director soon made his appearance and gave a short run-through of the day's activities. Adora looked giddy. This was probably the one destination she had expectations for, and she was convinced that the couple's relationship was to grow stronger, as the famous song promised. "Adora has listened to that song a million times, I hope Heidelberg lives up to it!" Ruben told the group while they waited in reception for disembarkation.

As with all cities in Germany, Heidelberg has been in existence for centuries. Archaeology proves that the city was first occupied in at least 1196 and developed at a rapid pace during the 13th century. In 1386, Germany's first university was built here, and stands as a monument to intellectualism. Heidelberg is often called the "City of Romanticism" due to its many buildings that were constructed in the Baroque style, a very elaborate style that symbolizes grandness (Heidelberg has a long story to tell, n.d.). The reason for this, however, is quite distressing. In the 17th century, the city was completely destroyed during a war with France, consequently leaving all medieval structures in ruins. It was on these ruins that Rococo City was built. It is possibly this style of architecture that gives one the impression of romance and inspired Henry Hall's famous composition. Additionally, the highly respected university drew many philosophers and poets to the area, giving it an atmosphere of learning and the supposed superiority of German culture. Maybe it was this sense of superiority that explained the strong support Heidelberg's residents had for the Nazi party. Throughout World War II, Heidelberg was sadly a stronghold for fascist propaganda due to the many intellectual powers residing there. Fortunately, the area was not faced with the level of destruction as that suffered by Cologne and retained many Baroque buildings that can still be enjoyed today. Since 1945, Heidelberg has become a city of science. This is rather odd as one is inclined to think that romance frequently has nothing to do with logical thinking or the scientific method! In the latter part of the 20th century, the university became a pilgrimage site of sorts for scientists around the world. There are about 80 research establishments, culminating in one of the most influential biotechnology centers around the world. Ruben and his group were more interested in history, and they were convinced to experience the romantic aspect of this city during their short visit.

Having said that, due to the historical significance of the university, the tour guide stressed the importance of visiting it first. Today, the university has a few campuses, and the group was to visit the "old university," which was built in the early 18th century. No lectures take place here, and the building is largely viewed as a museum, making it the perfect spot for a visit from a historical perspective. Before entering, the tour guide told the group that the influential composer Robert Schumann attended classes in the building. Ruby, a great lover of music, imagined Schumann walking through the doors they were now entering as well. "First, we see the great hall," the tour guide instructed. "This is where students in the 19th and early 20th centuries went for classes." To Ruben, it looked like Westminster Abbey in London, with similar pews on either side of the room. It was designed and built in 1886 to commemorate the institution's 500th anniversary. Ruben and Adora noticed the busts of the founders around the room, whereas Pol and Ruby were invested in the many paintings of these figures. "Follow me into the student prison," the tour guide said. The prison room sounded threatening to Ruben. Once they entered the room, it didn't seem unpleasant, quite cozy, in fact. The student prison was a detention room where disobeying students were sent between the 1780s and 1914. Scattered over the walls are engravings from former residents who stayed for periods ranging from two days to four weeks. "Were the students allowed to leave?" Adora asked the tour guide. "Yes, they still had to attend lectures but had to come back here as soon as their class ended." "Good thing we didn't study in the 19th century," Ruby remarked. Following the prison, they went to the university museum. Here, they saw exhibits detailing the university's history from 1386 to now. "We're about to leave for the Karl-Theodor Bridge," the tour guide said over Ruben's earpiece. He waved to Pol and Ruby, who were standing quite a distance from him and Adora, "Come on, it's time to go."

The Karl-Theodor Bridge is by no means an ancient structure like many others in Heidelberg. In fact, it is the ninth bridge that has stood at that location. Eight bridges were built over the Neckar River over a span of 700 years. However, they were all constructed with wood and other materials susceptible to damage. This was to change in 1784 when the older bridge collapsed and prompted Prince Karl-Theodor to build a new one that would stand through the ages. The current bridge was completed four years later. Today, it consists of nine arches and two towers topped with statues of Karl Theodor and the Roman deity Minerva. The skeleton of the bridge is made from sandstone that subsequently erodes when it comes in contact with water. Ultimately, this led the German government to seal it with cement for safety reasons in 2006. "I wonder if this bridge will be different from the one in Cologne," Adora asked Ruben as they neared it. Fortunately, it was completely different and looked like a museum in itself. The two statues over the bridge told a story, one of German history that Ruben thoroughly enjoyed. Pol and Ruby were looking at the statue of Karl Theodor when Ruben grabbed Adora's hand and stood by the railing. "Look at that little boat in the distance," Ruben pointed to an old wooden boat that seemed a century old. "If you close your eyes, you can almost sense the millions of people who have walked over this bridge in centuries past," Adora mentioned in a soft voice. Ruben had read up on this area and told her, "During World War II, the German troops bombed three of the arches." Ruben was correct. It almost destroyed the bridge, but Karl Theodor's efforts in building a strong structure paid off, and it was able to be restored after the war. When the group walked towards the old city, they saw a statue of a monkey holding a mirror. The tour guide interjected, "This monkey was placed here in 1979, but it's not the first of its kind. A monkey has always been present in some form since the 15th century." Ruben moved closer to have a look at this odd feature. "It is said that if you rub the monkey's mirror, you will become wealthy, and if you rub the fingers, you'll come back here someday." Adora was quick to rub everything so as to throw in her chances for both attractive eventualities! "Stand next to it, I'll take a photo of you," Ruben told her. Her shy smile made Ruben weak. He didn't even look at the monkey while taking the picture. "You look so beautiful," he said to himself.

Right over the bridge lies the Altstadt. This is the oldest part of the city and is overlooked by the castle. Ruben and his group walked into the area with great fascination. The narrow streets and cobblestone flooring are the closest one could get to a time machine. Their first stop was the Madonna at the center of the corn market. As the name suggests, the corn market was a place where agricultural vendors came to sell their produce. "It makes me think of Oliver Twist," Ruby said when they roamed the large square. The Madonna was placed there in 1718 and became a pilgrimage for Catholics in the region. "It's beautiful," Adora remarked while Ruben was again getting ready to take a photograph. Here, they also saw the town hall that was built in 1701, and the architecture is precisely what one would expect from the period. Ruben admired the abundance of elongated windows with a sense of respect for the builders who constructed it centuries prior. "I'm hungry," Pol said as they were standing about. "Let's have something ethnically German," Adora suggested. In Amsterdam, they certainly enjoyed Dutch cuisine, and in Germany, they would do the same. The tour guide soon interrupted their conversation, "If you make your way to the marketplace, you'll find many stalls with traditional German delicacies," This suggestion excited Ruben as his stomach was rumbling by now. One of the stalls had a sign that said, *Bratwurst* (German sausage). "Beer and sausage, that's what Germany is known for!" Ruby said. Each of them sampled one and loved it. Ruben noted that it tasted like nothing he's had in the United States before. Moreover, Adora liked it so much that she wanted another. "Don't get too full sampling Bratwurst, we still have a few things to try," Ruben mentioned. Next was schnitzel with sauerkraut at a store directly opposite where they were standing. Luckily, the vendor spoke English, and Ruben could ask that she give each a small piece just to taste. Everyone enjoyed the schnitzel, but Adora and Pol despised the sauerkraut. "What is in this, it tastes sour," Pol mentioned as he struggled to swallow it. Ruben and Ruby laughed at their reaction as they gobbled it down with delight. *Bienenstich*—bee sting— was their choice for dessert. The legend goes that this cake made from sweet yeast dough was served after bakers in the 15th century threw beehives at troublemakers who attempted to enter the village, hence the name. This too the group enjoyed thoroughly. Before making their way back to the Tialfi, Ruben made sure to buy a pretzel. "You can't come to Germany without trying one of these!"

Ruben and the group soon made their way back to the Tialfi, waiting for them in the Heidelberg harbor. As soon as Ruben saw the vessel, he felt a sense of relief. Of course, he and the others enjoyed touring each stop. But he yearned for personal time with Adora on the vessel. Every day they stopped somewhere and were required to disembark for a tour of the city or town. Similarly, Pol and Ruby were tired of the constant walking and were undoubtedly looking forward to boarding. This, by no stretch, meant that they were ungrateful for the opportunity to visit different countries. However, by now, they needed to rest and gather their thoughts about the vacation thus far. On their way back, the Cruise Director mentioned, "Say goodbye to land, tomorrow we're staying on board," Just what Ruben was waiting for. He and Adora could use a lazy day without the need to get up at a specified time as set forth by their tour guide. As Ruben entered the ship, he gave a loud sigh. Adora knew the reason for this. She also needed a day to recuperate. The objective for tomorrow was going to be relaxation. That was the only way they could appreciate their next two stops in their totality.

Chapter 8:
Day 6—Time for a Relaxing Day Onboard

The famous boat designer Francis Herreshoff once said, "A cabin is truly a wonderful thing; not only will it shelter you from a tempest, but from the other troubles of life, it is a safe retreat" (Wiedemann, 2020, p. 34). This is exactly how Ruben felt when he woke up on day six of their journey. He knew that today was going to be one filled with opportunities for some alone time with his beloved Adora. Waking up to the Rhine outside their window was certainly a dream come true. Yet, he much preferred looking at Adora, who was still fast asleep. How did he get so lucky? The thought entered his mind and never ceased to escape that morning. Today, they were on no schedule, and he could arrange it as he saw fit. He kept thinking of ways to make it special for Adora. Ruben was quick to recognize that everyone likes to be awakened with a cup of warm coffee. Ruben threw on his robe and slippers and walked to the coffee station, where he made them both a cappuccino. He was relieved when he entered the stateroom, and Adora was still asleep. "Good morning, beautiful," Ruben said as he held the cup of coffee in front of Adora's face. She was grateful and thanked him with an affectionate kiss. "I ordered breakfast to be sent to the room," Ruben followed. Adora wanted to eat on the balcony in order to take advantage of the breathtaking view. Even so, this was short-lived as the vessel was creeping slowly towards a river lock. The Tialfi had encountered these before, but it was the first time Ruben and Adora were actively focused on the process. The view was consequently replaced by big concrete walls on both sides! Adora felt a tad intimidated as the vessel maneuvered to reach the correct level of floatation before the gates opened to continue. "Well, that was something new," Adora said with a smile. "So, what do you want to do today?" Ruben eagerly asked. Adora didn't want to make plans. "Let's just see what happens," she replied.

For the first time, Ruben took a deeper look at the luxurious hallway when they walked towards the dining room for breakfast. It looked so clean and smelled fresh. One wouldn't think that this ship has been housing residents for a couple of years. On their way, they bumped into Ruby and Adora. "Good, today we're arriving in the dining room at the same time!" Pol remarked. By now, the group had a table that they preferred, in the corner right next to the window. Luckily, it was still available, and Adora ran in front of the group so as to reserve it for them. "Will you fetch us something from the buffet we can share?" Adora asked Ruben. He and Pol left the ladies at the table and filled their plates with all the delicacies they could find. Back at the table, Adora and Ruby were having a personal conversation surrounding Adora's thoughts on Ruben thus far. "He is so sweet, I think we have a long future awaiting us," Adora said. Ruby was elated and replied, "Ruben is a really good guy; I think you made the right choice of coming on this trip." Adora was delighted with her feedback. She had tremendous respect for Ruby and would seriously consider breaking off the relationship if Ruby did not approve. "Here are the plates," Ruben mentioned as he sat down with their meal. Ruben knew exactly what Adora liked to eat and filled it up with all her favorites. Similarly, Ruby was pleased with Pol's choices. While eating, Adora thought of Tess. This was the first time she had been apart from her aunt for such a long time, and she was feeling tender when thinking about her all alone in Florida. "Continue eating, I'm going to call Tess quickly," Adora said as she stood up and made her way outside. Tess was immensely grateful and asked her about the trip. "It's amazing; hopefully, I'll bring you here someday," Adora assured her. Tess consequently knew that Ruben was taking good care of her, and she had nothing to worry about.

After breakfast, Pol and Ruby opted to stay seated in the dining room. But Ruben and Adora went to the terrace to enjoy the view and the sunlight. Ruby shortly joined them and found a deck chair next to Adora. "The weather is phenomenal," she said when she sat down. From the terrace, they saw many sights on the banks of the Rhine. Ruben didn't know exactly where they were, but the castles and other historical buildings scattered about made it seem like they were in the center of Germany. He was correct. "Would you like a blanket?"

Ruben asked Adora as she seemed quite cold. "That would be marvelous," she replied. Ruben couldn't find a blanket close to them and ran to their stateroom to retrieve one. Adora had brought a soft blanket that Tess had made for her on the trip. She knew she was going to miss her and viewed it as a way of bringing a piece of her on the vacation. Ruben thought this would be the perfect choice and grabbed it before closing the door behind him. In the hallway, he bumped into a crew member. "Are you ready for the entertainment tonight?" he asked Ruben. "What entertainment?" Ruben inquired. "The German singer that will be joining us over dinner this evening." This greatly excited Ruben as he knew Adora loved dancing. *What better way to lift our spirits than with some slow dancing*, he thought. Back on the terrace, he gave Adora the special blanket. "It feels like I'm giving Tess a hug," she said while covering her shoulders with it. "I heard we're going to have some entertainment this evening," Ruben informed the ladies. Just as he said that, they witnessed a couple on a sailboat waving to them. Adora heard the man say something but couldn't make out what it meant. "It's probably German," Ruby explained.

"Where's Pol?" Ruben asked. Quite concerned about their friend's absence, Ruby went inside to look for him. Finally, she found Pol in the bar, sipping on an ice-cold lager. Seeing him alone made Ruby feel tender, and she soon asked Ruben and Adora to join them for a drink. Ruben had a lager as well, and the ladies ordered cocktails. "Why don't you have a lager as well, Adora?" Pol asked, knowing full well she despised it. Adora rolled her eyes, which made Ruben snicker. "How are you enjoying the trip?" the barman inquired. Adora told him how much they loved the Tialfi and how they appreciated the efforts of the crew to make them comfortable. The barman was delighted that their hard work was paying off and thanked her for her kind words. Pol's two lagers made him tired. "Alcohol always has this effect on me," he remarked. He and Ruby went to their stateroom for a nap, leaving Ruben and Adora alone at the bar. Now they had some personal time to talk about things not appropriate for their friend's ears! After a while, Ruben suggested they try out the mini-golf course after Adora finished her cocktail. She readily agreed to this proposition, and they soon set off on their onboard adventure. First, they roamed the walking track that extends around the full circumference of the vessel, looking at the sights from all sides of the Tialfi. Second, they located the mini-golf and started to play. "No cheating!" Adora yelled. To Ruben's amazement, Adora was quite talented at the game, and she won. "One for Adora, zero for Ruben!" she uttered with glee. Ruben didn't care. As long as he saw Adora happy, no competition would stand between him and his love for her. That being said, the quick succession of activities left both of them fatigued. They figured the best way to enjoy the entertainment that evening was to get some rest before dinner. In their stateroom, Ruben closed the blinds, and the two fell asleep as soon as their heads touched the pillows.

They were only awakened by a knock on the door. It was Ruby. "We only have 30 minutes until dinner starts," she said. "Did we sleep that long," Adora asked as she wiped her eyes. A look in the mirror had Adora in a state of worry. Her hair was messy, and her makeup was smudged. Ruben still thought she was breathtaking, but Adora knew that she needed to freshen up for the upcoming event. After a shower, Adora picked out something to wear, a black dress with heels. Similarly, Ruben dressed smartly for entertainment. Their outfits were much more formal than what they'd worn on the trip so far. "There's something about wearing nice clothes," Adora told Ruben while she applied her lipstick. "You look beautiful," Ruben said while resisting the temptation to stare. Entering the dining room, they could see a stand with musical equipment next to the buffet area. One instrument caught Adora's attention. It was a German accordion and looked so heavy that she couldn't imagine carrying it for the entire evening. The group picked a table close to the performance area and sat down for dinner. The food that evening was delicious and left Ruben stuffed. "Dancing will be a good workout after this meal," Pol said after taking his last bite. Adora did not eat as much so as to keep her energy for the dancing that was bound to happen anytime. Suddenly, a man and woman walked in dressed in traditional German attire. "That's Lederhosen," Ruben whispered to Adora when she looked perplexed about their outfits. Although it was different, Adora loved the traditional dress adorned by the female performer. Everybody turned their chairs to face the show. The performers' accents were very strong, resulting in the group being confused by some of what they were saying. Nevertheless, that wasn't important. "Music is a universal language!" Ruby exclaimed. They started playing *Volksmusik* - folk music - that was very upbeat and distinct from anything American. Ruben had never heard something like this before and was taken aback by the foreign tunes. Yet, with every new song, they began to enjoy it more. Perhaps every song seemed more amusing after every sip of champagne! By the fourth song, the group was totally immersed in the music, and Adora beckoned Ruben to join her on the dance floor. They weren't sure what style of dancing would be fitting for this genre of music. They simply followed the natural movements their body made. Ruben grabbed Adora and moved around the dance floor with her in his arms. They were the picture of the carefree nature that is young love. After the dance, Ruben and Adora left the dining room and stood outside. Holding on to the railing, Ruben took Adora's hand and softly said, "You're my forever person."

Chapter 9:
Day 7—Navigating Alsatian Culture in Strasbourg

"Bonjour," Adora said to Ruben when he awakened on the second-last day of their trip. For a moment, he didn't recognize why she would say this. But he was quick to remember that they were going to Strasbourg! The Tialfi was almost in the section of the Rhine occupied by France. Adora had studied French in school and wanted to practice the language she undoubtedly became rusty at. When Ruben read about Strasbourg back in the United States, he learned that the city is known as France's little Germany in that it resides on the border of the latter. At breakfast, Strasbourg was the main theme of the group's conversation. "I think Strasbourg is known as an Alsatian community," Pol remarked. He was correct. In fact, the whole region is known as Alsace, a term that has come to mean a mixture of French and German. Adora interjected, "Oh, it's almost like some areas in Canada where French and English are spoken equally." Yet, not only do Strasbourg residents *speak* French and German, but their customs have intertwined to such an extent that it is viewed as a distinct culture in itself. Because it lies on the border, there have been occasional outbreaks of conflict instigated by both countries, who believed that the city belonged to them. However, residents of Strasbourg are generally not patriotic about either one. Rather, they choose to take pride in their own unique culture and the many Alsace historical attractions peppered throughout the city. While in the dining room, the tour guide arrived and told the group about their upcoming activities for the day. "It's going to feel strange to leave the vessel; I was becoming comfortable with the river life from yesterday," Ruby noted. Nevertheless, Adora and Ruben were excited to do some sightseeing after a day of onboard recuperation. Unbeknownst to Adora, this was going to be her favorite stop of the entire cruise.

The area now known as Strasbourg was originally formed as a Celtic village but morphed into a city after the Romans conquered the region and implemented their style of government. This led to many migrants moving there, and the city grew exponentially. The Romans called it Argentoratum and used the Rhine River to their advantage about trade and economic development. Yet, residents grew uneasy with the Roman influence, and the city was overtaken by the Franks in the 5th century. The Franks were not a united group in that many cultures fell under the umbrella term. It was during this period that the Alsatian culture started to take form, as Louis II—king of the East Franks—signed an alliance with Charles II—king of the West Franks—in 842. The document that they signed is the oldest written in old French. However, they still fell under Roman rule, and the citizens in Strasbourg were unhappy with the authority given to Catholic bishops. The war that ensued made the city a free one while still technically under the control of the Roman Empire. This all changed in 1681 when the French King Louis XIV conquered the city, and it fell under French rule. By now, most people living there were protestant due to the Reformation, which was heavily influenced by one Strasbourg resident, John Calvin. The people were mostly pleased with their new form of government, but this was to change after the French Revolution, which resulted in the French authorities losing some control. Strasbourg residents were quite patriotic in their French heritage, and the famous Claude-Joseph Rouget de Lisle soon penned La *Marseillaise*—the current national anthem of France—in 1792. Almost 100 years later, Germany annexed the city during the Franco-German War but lost it after their defeat in World War I. Again, during World War II, Strasburg was occupied by Nazi Germany and once again became French after 1945. Today, Strasbourg is the seat of the European Parliament, A city that stands as a symbol of European unity.

At breakfast, Ruben and his group saw the cathedral in the distance and were told by the Cruise Director that this was going to be the main attraction. Nevertheless, on their way to the cathedral, they were going to see many famous attractions, such as the Palais Rohan and Quartier Krutenau. "Come, Adora, take my hand,"

Ruben said as they left the Tialfi. Perhaps the previous day of inactivity left her confused as to how to approach the gangway! Although the harbor is not far from the cathedral, the tour guide encouraged the group to take the tour bus for a faster journey. Additionally, he would be able to tell them a bit about the locations they were to see from the bus windows. "Look! It is the French Buckingham Palace!" Adora yelled when they passed the Palais Rohan. The tour guide instructed, "The palace was built in the 1730s and entertained notable figures from French history, such as Marie Antoinette." "Wasn't she the queen that lost her head at the guillotine?" Ruby asked. The tour guide seemed a bit uncomfortable with the gruesome demise of the queen and simply nodded his head in agreement. When they were close to their destination, the bus suddenly stopped. "Why are we stopping? We're not at the cathedral, are we?" Pol asked those around him. The tour guide explained, "In order to reach the cathedral, we're going to walk through Rue Mercière [Merchant Street]." At first, Ruben and Adora were irked by the idea that they had to walk through a busy street. But it soon became clear that it was a sight in itself. This street dates back to the medieval age and reminded Ruben of the Marksburg castle. The old cobblestones and buildings were reminiscent of the period. "The Marksburg Castle was where the medieval nobles lived, and this street is where the average person roamed," Ruben said. "So, in other words, this is where people like us would have wandered a thousand years ago," Ruby said with a smirk. The group laughed at the supposed disrespect Ruby just displayed for their social status. "Adora would have been at Marksburg because her beauty is fitting for a queen," Ruben said with a wink. "Get a room!" Pol jokingly replied. The group was soon at the front door of the cathedral, all the while snickering at their conversation.

The Strasbourg Cathedral is a highlight for all tourists who visit the area. The Gothic architecture is spectacular, and the level of detail is impeccable. Before entering, the group was fixated on the many features inundating the outer walls. While in the midst of wonder, the tour guide gave some history of the building. "Construction of the structure began in 1015 and only ended in 1049 when it was consecrated by Pope Leo IX." Ruben was even more enchanted after learning that the building is over 1000 years old! The tour guide continued, "After construction finished, it was the highest building in the world for 400 years and was even a Protestant stronghold for a while until it was reabsorbed by the Catholics in 1681." The sculptures of the prophets on the outside had Ruben wondering whether this was what they really looked like. Sure, he's read about them in the Bible, but seeing them up close was a different experience. Once they entered, their amazement grew even greater. Right in front of them, down the aisle, was the Rose Window. This stained-glass window is said to represent the omnipresent nature of God, perpetually overlooking His creation. The beauty of the window gave Adora a lump in her throat. "I wonder how long it took the artists to make this." She whispered to Ruben. He did not have an answer but was sure it would take them many years. The pulpit below the window was built in 1486. "This is made from white sandstone and shows many sculptures that clearly indicate the Gothic approach to art," the tour guide commented. "Where are Pol and Ruby?" Ruben asked when he turned around. They were standing below the organ. Ruby beckoned Adora to join them. The organ is covered with sculptures of Bible characters and is flanked by two breathtaking stained-glass windows. They were told that an organ had been present in the cathedral since about 1260 but was rebuilt in 1489, which is the one we see today. Similarly, the astronomical clock was also an intriguing sight to see. The clock is not as old as other features, as it was built in the 19th century. But it remains a favorite for tourists who visit the building. When the clock chimed, Ruben and Adora saw sculptures of Jesus and his apostles move positions. "How are they able to move like that?" Adora asked Ruben. Ruben, being no engineer, didn't have an answer and pointed to something else: The staircase. The tour guide saw Ruben's wandering eyes and asked them if they would like to make their way upwards to the North Tower. Surprisingly, Pol and Ruby were going to join them on their climb! Before they started their ascent, the tour guide mentioned, "Make sure to look for the Black Forest; this is where "Hansel and Gretel" supposedly took place." Ruben and Adora saw no children throwing breadcrumbs or a candy house in the distance, but it remained a beautiful sight. Ruben situated himself behind Adora and held her by the waist while they enjoyed the view. "We should probably get going; I think we're going to the Old Town now." Ruben noted.

"Everyone outside," Ruben heard over his earpiece. The tour guide was calling them to the exit. "We're going to give you two hours to walk around the old town and experience this wonderful community on your own," he said. Adora was grateful for the chance to tour without strange companions for a short while. Pol and Ruby said they would go a separate way and so left the lovebirds to explore on their own. Ruben didn't show it, but he was immensely grateful for this gesture. Their first stop was called "Jew Street." Ruben saw the remnants of a thriving Jewish community that is unfortunately no longer present. Yet, their memory is forever ingrained in the many buildings from the period they lived there. This street was now peppered by many small boutiques that interested Adora. Following this, they walked through *Grand'Rue*. This street is the oldest in the city, and the wood-paneled buildings reminded the couple that they were truly in Europe. To them, it looked more like Germany than France, and the Alsace culture became clearer. Moreover, on this street are several bakeries that offer Arabic specialties. Ruben didn't want to get something here, rather choosing to wait for an Alsace option they were bound to discover. As soon as this thought entered his mind, they walked into Place Kléber, an area surrounded by buildings from the late 19th century. Here, they saw a plaque that detailed its history.

"Place Kléber was the arena of many public executions by guillotine," Ruben read. Adora didn't want to think of the many heads that rolled here! Instead, she saw a restaurant that seemed Alsace in nature and asked Ruben to join her for lunch.

The restaurant was called *Au Vieux Strasbourg*. Their tour guide had told them about the Alsace atmosphere in this restaurant, and the couple was relieved to find it so easily by themselves. Fortunately, the busy restaurant had an open seat. The atmosphere was warm, and the many paintings on the wall made it seem like a museum of sorts. They were not only going to eat ethnic cuisine, but they were engulfed in the culture of Strasbourg by simply sitting there! The waiter was friendly and welcomed them to the city. Adora tried out her French but was quick to realize that her language skills were wholly inadequate to communicate with the waiter. He spoke some English and showed them a page on the menu with traditional Alsatian meals. Ruben opted to have the stew of pike perch and potatoes, whereas Adora ordered the potatoes with Muenster and peasant bacon. While eating, Ruben noted that this was one of the nicest meals he's had on the trip so far. "I agree, this bacon is exquisite," Adora replied. The meal was completed with the couple ordering traditional Alsace coffee. Knowing that they needed to be back at a certain time, they had to make haste in order to see a few more attractions around the town. Next to the restaurant was a souvenir shop. "Let's go in there; I need to get something for Tess," Adora said. While Adora was looking around, Ruben took some photographs of her looking at the merchandise. She chose to buy three postcards that had Strasbourg written on them. Ruben almost bought a little teddy bear but reminded himself that there was no space left in his luggage! As they left the shop, they realized it's been two hours. "We need to run," Ruben said urgently. For a moment, the couple was lost but luckily found their way back to the bus in a matter of minutes. "This is going to be our last evening on the Tialfi," Ruben mentioned to Adora. This statement seemed to make her sad. But at the same time, she was eager to see Tess and be at home again. "This certainly won't be our last trip, so I wouldn't worry if I were you," Ruben continued in a soothing tone. Holding hands, Ruben and Adora embarked on the Tialfi with their friends by their side. They were all to spend their final night on this magnificent vessel.

Chapter 10:

Day 8—A Swiss Disembarkation in Basel

Amit Kalantri once said, "If the earth is a mother, then rivers are her veins" (Durga, 2020, p. 138). This was the case for Ruben and his group. They spent eight days sailing through one of the biggest veins in Europe: The Rhine. Their last evening on the Tialfi was bittersweet. Pol and Ruby decided to eat in their stateroom, opting to spend their last evening together. Perhaps they did this to give Ruben and Adora some personal time to properly celebrate the end of their journey. Adora seemed a tad despondent. "Are you okay?" Ruben asked with a semblance of worry. "Nothing's wrong; I'm just a bit sad because we're going home soon," she replied. Ruben could understand this. He was also feeling quite gloomy that the trip was to come to an end. "Look at the lights outside," he told Adora. She looked up, her hair gracefully changing position. The darkness of the night was periodically interrupted by lights from a building onshore. "We saw so many countries and sights that will last a lifetime of memories," Ruben said, "I wouldn't have wanted to spend it with anyone else but you." Adora moved in and gave him a kiss. This seemed to lift her spirits. "Although we'll be leaving Europe tomorrow, I'll be with you every step of the way," Ruben continued. Adora gave a deep sigh of relief. She knew that Ruben was the man for her and that this trip was only the beginning of the true journey of love they were going to explore once back in the United States. Trying to lift her spirits further, Ruben suggested they have a drink at the bar and then sit on the terrace, breathing the fresh night air. "Let's go outside," Adora said even before reaching the bar. It was there that Adora grabbed him and kissed Ruben passionately. "I love you so much," she told him as the Rhine River flowed beneath them. Their trip was almost forgotten, and the couple was only focused on the deep affection they had for each other. Before going to bed, Ruben assured her, "Remember, we're still going to visit Switzerland tomorrow!" Adora closed her eyes and fell asleep in Ruben's arms.

The following morning, Pol and Ruby joined them at breakfast. "I hope I'll be able to sleep as comfortably at home like I did on the Tialfi!" Pol remarked while eating. Ruben put more on his plate than he had on the previous days, seemingly in an attempt to try everything he had not yet tasted. Adora said that she wasn't hungry and only had a cup of coffee. Ruby asked her if she wanted to go to the terrace for one last look at the landscape. The women soon left the table, leaving Ruben and Pol alone at the table. "Thank you for suggesting this trip, Ruben," Pol said. "It was something I thought I would never experience." Ruben felt a sense of pride in instigating the vacation plans. "Anything for Adora," he replied. Pol was convinced that Ruben was the right partner for his friend, and he readily let him know. Not only was this trip one to strengthen Ruben's relationship with Adora, but he was now friends with two of the most important people in her life. Outside, Adora and Ruby were looking at Switzerland lying on the banks of the river. "Attention, please," the Cruise Director said as he entered the dining room. Adora and Ruby rushed back in and found their seats. "Firstly, the crew of the Tialfi would like to thank you for entrusting us with your vacation." All the tourists clapped so as to thank them in return. He continued, "We hope you enjoyed it onboard and learned a lot from our guides on land." Again, everyone clapped. "We will soon reach Basel, after which you will have three hours to tour the city." For a moment, Ruben was wondering what would happen with their luggage or where they should board the bus to the airport. His concerns were quickly addressed. "You will all have the ability to board the vessel after the tour and gather your things before getting on the bus a short distance from here." All the tourists were to congregate at a specific spot that was to be identified when they disembarked with their luggage. After a run to their staterooms, the group was ready to tour Basel. "Let's make our last trip one for the books!" Ruben encouraged.

As Strasbourg, the city of Basel can trace its roots back to the Celts. The Romans founded a port here in 44 BCE, calling it "Basileia." However, after the fall of the Roman Empire, the region came to be inhabited by the French Allemans. It was during this period that the area became a stronghold of Catholicism under the leadership of various bishops. They spearheaded many urban developments, with the introduction of numerous cathedrals and other features, such as the city wall. The Rhine River was a meeting point for many during this era, which subsequently led to the first bridge being built in 1225. The mid-14th century was a time of turmoil for Basel residents. First, they were hit with the Black Plague, which killed the majority of residents. Only to be followed by the immeasurable suffering posed by a devastating earthquake in 1356. Sadly, many Jewish residents were believed to be the instigators of these calamities and were killed in various massacres after the events. A century later, the city was rebuilt and consequently invigorated by Christian leadership after the Council of Basel was formed. Similarly, it was a source of pride for the Catholic Church after Pope Pius II founded a university there. Yet, the Reformation stripped the Catholics of power and transformed the city into a Protestant stronghold. Many cultural achievements were made in the quest for knowledge due to the prevalence of the influential university. Protestants from all over Europe made their way to Basel and established it as a commercial entity after the introduction of the profitable silk trade. Every day, ships sailed on the Rhine, trading in this precious material. The Industrial Revolution was thus paramount in the city's development, and Basel was the location of the first railway in Switzerland, built in 1844. Miraculously, the city was spared during the First and Second World Wars and was relatively protected from the destruction occurring outside of its borders. After the airport Basel-Mulhouse was built in 1953, the city became known as an international attraction. Today, Basel remains a must-see visit for tourists to Switzerland.

On the Tialfi, Ruben and Adora were packing their bags frantically so as not to miss the few hours they had to tour Basel. "Did you pack the postcards you bought in Strasbourg?" Ruben asked Adora. She nodded and made sure that everything was neatly arranged, even assisting Ruben when she disapproved of his packing style! Adora was concerned that her luggage might be overweight due to the many souvenirs she bought at their various stops. "We should get going, Pol and Ruby are probably waiting for us in reception," Ruben beckoned Adora to leave the room. While waiting for her in the hallway, he saw one of the crew members who had brought the couple their room service meals several times. Ruben called her. "Thank you for your kindness," Ruben said with a smile. She was appreciative and wished him well, "I hope we'll see you again!" Leaving the Tialfi, Pol asked the group, "Where should we go?" The tour guide did not accompany them today, leaving the group somewhat lost with regard to what they should do. "I read up on the *Marktplatz* in a brochure last night," Adora mentioned. Ruben agreed that this was a good choice because it would give them an inkling of the long history of the city. The marketplace was a short distance from the Tialfi and was reached by the group in no more than five minutes.

Once there, they walked along the various streets behind the market where artisans lived for centuries. "Look at the old houses," Adora mentioned. Many of the buildings date back to the 15th century and maintained their beauty throughout the many historical events. Overpowering the marketplace was the town hall, which had been standing for 500 years. The red concrete walls were unusual. "Where have you seen a red building like this in the United States?" Ruby asked. Moreover, the red façade was painted with religious figures that culminated in the unique clock located in the middle. The clock has been in operation since 1512 and has never missed a day of work. "Perhaps the religious figures atop have protected it from wear and tear!" Ruben remarked. Below the clock was a statue of a man who was unknown to the group at first glance. When they moved closer, however, they read that it was a statue of Munatius Plancus, the founder of the town. Ruben took Adora's hand and walked to the Tinguely Fountain. The fountain was built in 1977 and consists of iron figures that periodically jet streams of water into the air. It proved to be the perfect spot to end the visit. Pol and Ruby sat on a bench nearby. "This trip was wonderful," Adora told Ruben in a solemn tone. "You made it wonderful," Ruben replied. Holding hands, they watched on as the water spurted into the air. Ruben called Pol. "Could you take a picture of us?" he asked. With Ruben's arm now around Adora's waist, Pol snapped a photograph of the pair just as a splash of water jerked in their direction. The perfect photograph to end one of the best weeks of Ruben's life.

"All good things must come to an end" is a quote attributed to the 14th-century English poet Geoffrey Chaucer (Carlson & Dermer, 2016, p. 1685). From the surface, Ruben and Adora agreed with this quote. Of course, the cruise was coming to an end, giving one the impression of finality. Yet, Chaucer did not account for the fact that some good things might come to an end in order for other good things to flourish. Ruben and Adora's relationship flourished as a direct result of the trip and was only to grow further after their European tour came to a close. It was this thinking that prevented the couple from feeling despair at the thought of leaving. A quick trip back to the Tialfi allowed them to greet the many employees of the vessel who had become friends. Pol told one crew member that they'll definitely see them again when he and Ruby made the trip alone in the future. Adora gave one last look at their cozy stateroom as they walked out. On the bus to the airport, Ruben held Adora in his arms while she leaned over and watched Switzerland glide past. "This was an amazing journey," she whispered. Ruben caressed her hair and gave her a kiss on the cheek. The group opted to have lunch at a restaurant at the airport after checking in their luggage. Their conversation was inundated with what each person enjoyed most. Pol enjoyed Amsterdam, Ruby liked Heidelberg, and Adora admired Strasbourg and Kinderdijk. When everyone was looking at Ruben, awaiting his answer, he didn't pick a certain destination. "Everywhere I go with Adora is a dream," he said shyly. Adora smiled and gave him a hug. Pol and Ruby looked at each other, seemingly pleased at the high esteem Ruben held for their closest friend. As the plane began its ascent back to Florida, Adora looked at Ruben. "Thank you for everything," she said. Ruben took her hand; "Don't thank me yet; this is only the beginning!"

Conclusion

John O' Donohue once said, "I would love to live like a river flows, carried by the surprise of its own unfolding" (Higgs & McCarthy, 2008, p. 124). Ruben and Adora— together with Pol and Ruby—lived on the Rhine for eight days, consistently surprised by its unfolding. Their trip set the course for Ruben's relationship with his beloved Adora. As the Tialfi traversed the mighty Rhine, they were in a perpetual state of amazement by all the sights on the banks requesting their attention. Their trip proved to be the platform on which love prospered, and their quest for historical knowledge was fed on a daily basis. Every destination brought something new that each of them could savor and take back to the United States. This trip was by no means something Ruben had always planned to do. However, his admiration of Adora convinced him to make the reservation, and he never came to regret this decision. In Amsterdam, they saw the Koniklik Paleis and the canals that make this city a favorite for tourists around the world. The windmills in Kinderdijk were the perfect location for love to thrive due to the romantic nature of their sails flapping in the wind. Ruben did not expect much from Kinderdijk, but it was undoubtedly one of his favorites throughout the trip! The cathedral in Cologne was like nothing they'd ever seen before and strengthened not only their relationship but their strong Christian faith. On the other hand, the Marksburg castle in Koblenz brought Ruben and his group the closest to a time machine in that they walked through a real preserved medieval structure. The bridge in Heidelberg was phenomenal and ensured the couples' return to Europe as Adora indulged in the superstitious nature of the monkey statue!

In Strasbourg, they witnessed the mix of German and French culture by walking the old town and trying cuisine one could have nowhere else in the world. Their brief visit to Switzerland was worth the wait and ended the vacation on a high note. All this was furthered by their stay on the luxurious Tialfi that guaranteed safe and comfortable travel. Notwithstanding, the food, onboard activities, and tour guide services on land all being faultless. As soon as they reached the United States, Ruben and Adora could not stop talking about Europe and the many experiences they had together. Ruben even made a picture book for Adora so as to cement their visit for the ages. Adora looked through this countless times as she often felt nostalgic for the alluring landscape that is Europe. A few weeks after their trip, Ruben and Adora had a discussion over dinner. "Remember how much we loved the Rhine?" he asked Adora affectionately. Adora knew he had something up his sleeve. "Yes?" she replied. "Well, I've been reading up on the Danube River and think we better go next time." Adora was speechless but overjoyed with his proposition. The couple was to fly over the pond again once more. We'll see you on the couple's next European cruise!

References

Amsterdam Museum. (n.d.). 10Best. https://www.10best.com/destinations/netherlands/amsterdam/spui/attractions/amsterdam-museum/

Amsterdam Port Map and Cruise Schedule. (n.d.). CruiseMapper. https://www.cruisemapper.com/?poi=56

Carlson, J., & Dermer, S. B. (2016). *The SAGE Encyclopedia of Marriage, Family, and Couples Counseling.* SAGE Publications.

A circuit through the castle – a step into history! (n.d.). Marksburg. https://www.marksburg.de/en/circuit/#/

Dana, C. A. (1869). *The Household Book of Poetry.* D. Appleton.

De Cleen, M. (2022, April 14). *Inside the Palace on Dam square.* MforAmsterdam. https://mforamsterdam.com/inside-the-palace-on-dam-square/#:~:text=(July%202021).

Durga, R. T. (2020). *The Eco-Quote Book.* Blue Hill Publications

A Dutch dinner party! (n.d.). The Dutch Table. https://www.thedutchtable.com/2013/02/a-dutch-dinner-party.html

Dutch snacks. (n.d.). IamExpat. https://www.iamexpat.nl/lifestyle/dutch-food-cuisine-dishes/snacks

The Fortress City of Koblenz. (n.d.). Visit Koblenz. https://www.visit-koblenz.de/en/experience-koblenz/fortress-city

Garth. (2022, August 5). *Kinderdijk Windmills - A Day Trip From Rotterdam, Netherlands.* Phil and Garth. https://www.philandgarth.com/kinderdijk-windmills-a-day-trip-from-rotterdam/#7_Best_Things_To_Do_At_Kinderdijk

5 things you didn't know about the windmills at Kinderdijk. (2019, June 26). Cultural Cruises Europe. https://www.culturalcruiseseurope.com/blog/5-things-you-didnt-know-about-the-windmills-at-kinderdijk/

Hall, H. (1932). *I Lost My Heart in Heidelberg.* Spotify. https://open.spotify.com/track/5is1CZYHudwneoHULRwr2y

Heidelberg Bridge Monkey. (2017, September 11). Atlas Obscura. https://www.atlasobscura.com/places/heidelberg-bridge-monkey-heidelberger-bruckenaffe

Heidelberg has a long story to tell. (n.d.). Heidelberg. https://www.heidelberg.de/english/Home/Lif

e/History.html#:~:text=Heidelberg%20is%20t
he%20city%20of

Higgs, B., & McCarthy, M. (2008). *Emerging Issues II: The Changing Roles and Identities of Teachers and Learners in Higher Education*. NAIRTL.

History of Amsterdam. (n.d.). Amsterdam Info. https://www.amsterdam.info/basics/history/#:~:text=Amsterdam%20was%20founded%20as%20a

Hotel Restaurant Resslirytti. (n.d.). Resslirytti.ch. https://www.resslirytti.ch/en/around-basel/history/

Karl-Theodor Bridge. (n.d.). World Monuments Fund. https://www.wmf.org/project/karl-theodor-bridge

Koblenz, Germany. (n.d.). Britannica. https://www.britannica.com/place/Koblenz-Germany#ref2233

Koeln. (2012, July 23). *Cologne's Love Locks Bridge.* Atlas Obscura. https://www.atlasobscura.com/places/love-padlocks-cologne-s-hohenzollernbruecke-bridge

Kornmarkt with Madonna statue. (n.d.). ArrivalGuides. https://www.arrivalguides.com/en/Travelguide/Heidelberg/doandsee/kornmarkt-with-madonna-statue-8739

Kroeger, K. (2022, April 22). *Strasbourg Cathedral: A Visitor's Guide to this UNESCO Site*. Via Travelers. https://viatravelers.com/strasbourg-cathedral/

Lorelei. (n.d.). Encyclopedia Britannica. https://www.britannica.com/topic/Lorelei-German-legend

Macmillan, S. (2020, February 13). *What's new in the 2020 European river-cruise season*. Traveller. https://www.traveller.com.au/whats-new-in-the-2020-european-rivercruise-season-h1lq6b

Marcel Wanders: Interview by Blouin Artinfo. (n.d.). Reflexamsterdam. https://reflexamsterdam.com/press/marcel-wanders-interview-by-blouin-artinfo

Marktplatz (Market Square) in Basel, Switzerland. (n.d.). GPSmyCity. https://www.gpsmycity.com/attractions/markt platz-(market-square)-41176.html

Marksburg Castle, Braubach, Germany. (n.d.). Spotting History. https://www.spottinghistory.com/view/3697/marksburg-castle/

Mavrokefalidis, D. (2022, August 11). *Critical coal barges at deadlock as Rhine is set to be "impassable" by Friday*. Energy Live News. https://www.energylivenews.com/2022/08/11

/critical-coal-barges-at-deadlock-as-rhine-is-set-to-be-impassable-by-friday/

Medieval Torture Techniques - a top 7. (2020, February 19). King Richard III Visitor Centre. https://kriii.com/medieval-torture-techniques/

Menu at Loetje Amsterdam aan 't IJ, Amsterdam, Werfkade 14. (n.d.). Restaurant Guru. https://restaurantguru.com/Loetje-aan-t-IJ-Amsterdam/menu

Menu gourmandise du restaurant Au Vieux Strasbourg. (2014, May 30). Vieuxstrasbourg.fr. https://vieuxstrasbourg.fr/menu/

Nadeau, S. (2020, February 16). *Everything You Must Know About Visiting Cologne Cathedral.* Solosophie. https://www.solosophie.com/cologne-cathedral/

The Netherlands. (n.d.). Yad Vashem. https://www.yadvashem.org/righteous/stories/netherlands-historical-background.html

Nichols, B. (2009). *Rhapsody in Green: The Garden Wit and Wisdom of Beverley Nichols.* Timber Press.

NS-Documentation Centre. (n.d.). Museen Koeln. https://museenkoeln.de/portal/NS-Documentation-Centre

Old town around the Cathedral. (2016, June 16). Strassburg.eu.

http://www.strassburg.eu/en/old-town-strasbourg

Old University - Universität Heidelberg. (n.d.). Uni-Heidelberg.de. https://www.uni-heidelberg.de/en/university/history/old-university

Oude Kerk. (n.d.). 10Best. https://www.10best.com/destinations/netherlands/amsterdam/old-center-red-light-district/attractions/oude-kerk/

Perry, J. (2013). *The Insiders' Guide to Becoming a Yacht Stewardess 2nd Edition: Confessions from My Years Afloat with the Rich and Famous.* Morgan James Publishing.

Rhine Getaway. (n.d.). Viking. https://www.vikingrivercruises.com/cruise-destinations/europe/rhine-getaway/2024-amsterdam-basel/pricing.html#noscroll

Rhine River. (n.d.). Geography Name. https://geography.name/rhine-river/

Shams, K. (2021, December 12). 50 Best Windmill Quotes and Sayings on Living Free. Greeting Ideas. https://greetingideas.com/famous-windmill-quotes-sayings/

16 Top Tourist Attractions in Basel & Easy Day Trips. (n.d.). PlanetWare.

https://www.planetware.com/tourist-attractions-/basel-basle-bale-ch-bs-bas.htm

Strasbourg, France. (2019). In Encyclopædia Britannica. https://www.britannica.com/place/Strasbourg

Tower ascent. (n.d.). Cologne Tourism. https://www.cologne-tourism.com/see-experience/cologne-cathedral/tower-ascent/

Viking River Cruises. (n.d.). AffordableTours. https://www.affordabletours.com/rivers/viking/#:~:text=On%20average%20a%20river%20cruise

Viking Tialfi deck 2 plan. (n.d.). CruiseMapper. https://www.cruisemapper.com/deckplans/Viking-Tialfi-1192/deck02-2468

Wedia. (n.d.). *Cologne (Köln), Germany.* IamExpat. https://www.iamexpat.de/lifestyle/german-cities/cologne-koeln-city-guide

What is a muster drill? (n.d.). Royal Caribbean Cruises. https://www.royalcaribbean.com/faq/questions/muster-drill-onboard-safety#:~:text=A%20muster%20drill%20is%20a

Wiedemann, M. A. (2020). *Pocket Cruising and Micro Adventures: A simple sailing life - on a budget.* Books on Demand.

Wisboom pumping station. (n.d.). Kinderdijk Molens. https://www.kinderdijk.com/activities/wisboo m-pumping-station/

Made in the USA
Monee, IL
13 July 2023

39132179R00063